INSIGHT GUIDES

FLORENCE
StepbyStep

APA PUBLICATIONS
Part of the Langenscheidt Publishing Group

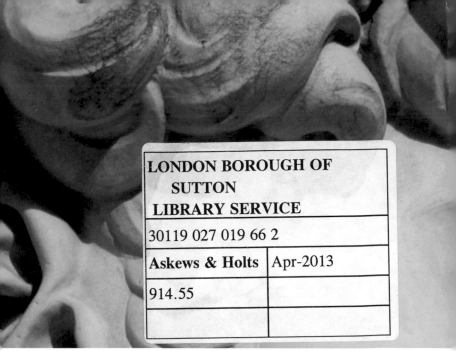

CONTENTS

ABOUT THIS BOOK

Above: the Duomo; local traffic; the Ponte Vecchio; Boboli Garden; San Miniato al Monte.

This *Step by Step Guide* has been produced by the editors of Insight Guides, whose books have set the standard for visual travel guides since 1970. With top-quality photography and authoritative recommendations, this guidebook brings you the very best of Florence in a series of 15 tailor-made tours.

WALKS AND TOURS

The tours in the book provide something to suit all budgets, tastes and trip lengths. As well as covering Florence's many classic attractions, the routes track lesser-known sights and up-and-coming areas; there are also excursions for those who want to extend their visit outside the city. The tours embrace a range of interests, so whether you are an art fan, a gourmet, a lover of flora and fauna or have children to entertain, you will find an option to suit.

We recommend that you read the whole of a tour before setting out. This should help you to familiarise yourself with the route and enable you to plan where to stop for refreshments – options for this are shown in the 'Food and Drink' boxes, recognisable by the knife-and-fork sign, on most pages.

For our pick of the walks by theme, consult Recommended Tours For... *(see pp.6–7).*

OVERVIEW

The tours are set in context by this introductory section, giving an overview of the city to set the scene, plus background information on food and drink, shopping and entertainment. A succinct history timeline highlights the key events that have shaped Florence over the centuries.

DIRECTORY

Also supporting the tours is a Directory chapter, comprising a user-friendly, clearly organised A–Z of practical information, our pick of where to stay while you are in the city and select restaurant listings; these eateries complement the more low-key cafés and restaurants that feature within the tours and are intended to offer a wider choice for evening dining. Also included here are select nightlife listings for evening entertainment.

The Authors

Maria Lord is a writer and editor, specialising in the arts and travel (particularly Tuscany, Central Europe, Greece and India). With her Tuscan partner she often travels to Florence and knows its art and architecture, and especially food and drink, extremely well.

This new edition was updated by Susie Boulton, a travel writer and art historian who has been a regular visitor to Florence for some 30 years. She first fell in love with Florence and Tuscany as a student, selling ice creams to pay for accommodation. She is the author of a dozen guides to Italy.

Some of the tours in this book were originally conceived by Christopher Catling.

Margin Tips
Shopping tips, historical facts, handy hints and information on activities help visitors to make the most of their time in Florence and its environs.

Feature Boxes
Notable topics are highlighted in these special boxes.

Key Facts Box
This box gives details of the distance covered on the tour, plus an estimate of how long it should take. It also states where the route starts and finishes, and gives key travel information such as which days are best to do the route, or handy transport tips.

Tour Map
Detailed cartography shows the tour clearly plotted with numbered dots. For more detailed mapping, see the pull-out map slotted inside the back cover.

Food and Drink
Recommendations of where to stop for refreshment are given in these boxes. The numbers prior to each restaurant/café name link to references in the main text. Restaurants in the Food and Drink boxes are plotted on the maps.

The € signs at the end of each entry reflect the approximate cost of a two-course meal for one, with a glass of house wine. These should be seen as a guide only. Price ranges, also quoted on the inside back flap for easy reference, are:

€€€€	60 euros and above
€€€	40–60 euros
€€	25–40 euros
€	25 euros and below

Footers
Look here for the tour name, a map reference and the main attraction on the double-page.

ART ENTHUSIASTS

Don't miss the Uffizi Gallery, showcasing the world's best collection of Renaissance art (walk 3), or the Accademia (walk 6), home to Michelangelo's *David*. Walk 4 covers both the Bargello (great for sculpture) and Santa Croce, famed for its frescoes by Giotto and Gaddi.

RECOMMENDED TOURS FOR...

CHILDREN

Keep the little ones amused in the Boboli Garden (walk 9), the Children's Museum (walk 2) or the Archaeological Museum (walk 6), where they can admire the mummies. If all else fails, treat them to ice cream at Grom (walk 1) or Gelateria Vivoli (walk 4).

ESCAPING THE CROWDS

If the historic centre seems oppressively crowded, take a day trip to hilltop Fiesole (tour 11), long a retreat for the city's residents. Tour 12, which visits Medici villas, also takes you off the beaten track.

FOOD AND WINE

Good tours for foodies include no. 5, which heads to the Mercato Centrale, where the ground floor is busy with food stalls and cafés. Walk 7 ends at one of the city's most popular tripe stands – not for the faint-hearted, but certainly authentic.

LITERATURE BUFFS

Marvel at the Baptistry, where Dante was christened and whose spectacular mosaics inspired him in his portrayal of hell, on walk 1. Visit Santa Croce on walk 4, as described in E.M. Forster's *A Room with a View*.

MEDICI FLORENCE

Walk 2 visits the Palazzo Vecchio, erstwhile home of the Medici, while their family tombs can be seen in the Medici Chapels, included in walk 5. Tour 12 takes you out of the city centre to focus on several villas built for the Medici.

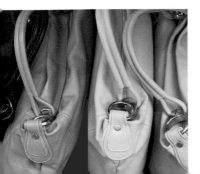

PARKS AND GARDENS

The city's main park, the Boboli Garden, is a highlight of walk 9. Attractions within the Boboli include statuary, grottoes and formal gardens, as well as the Pitti Palace, located just behind. The Medici Villas, visited on tour 12, are also notable for their lovely gardens.

RIVAL CITIES

There are several easy day trips from Florence. These include long-time rivals Siena (tour 14), Pisa (tour 15) and San Gimignano (tour 13) – an extraordinary hilltop village and the best-preserved medieval settlement in the country.

SHOPPING

Pop into the Mercato Centrale on walk 5 for local shopping (especially food). Alternatively, take a stroll along Via de' Tornabuoni, the city's most prestigious shopping street, and then end at the Mercato Nuovo, on walk 7.

VIEWS

Some of the best views of the city can be had from Piazzale Michelangelo and the church of San Miniato al Monte, visited on walk 10. There are also lovely views from the Boboli Garden (walk 9). For splendid panoramas of the Tuscan countryside, make for the village of Fiesole (tour 11).

OVERVIEW

An overview of Florence's geography, development and culture, plus illuminating background information on food and drink, shopping, entertainment and history.

INTRODUCTION

Famous for its contributions to science, literature, art and architecture, the city state of Florence is where the modern world began, and today it still retains a lively mix of dissent and luxury, the sublime and the earthy.

In most people's minds the name of Florence is indelibly linked to that of the Renaissance, when the extraordinarily rich flowering of artistic and intellectual life under the enlightened rule of the Medici, coupled with the city's immense banking wealth, made it the most important centre in Europe.

Florence Today

Contemporary Florence is without doubt one of the finest open-air museums in the world, and the tourism that this fuels has itself become a major new source of wealth. Rarely, however, is it considered as a city in contemporary terms, except perhaps for its shopping. Yet even here, the fine handicrafts and stylish fashion accessories for which it is now almost equally famous are ultimately rooted in Florence's own early mercantile and creative traditions.

Yet struggling to break free of its historical straitjacket is another, more hidden Florence, which, when the surface is scratched, reveals itself to be a sophisticated, tuned-in, complex and even slightly troubled modern city, and anything but one suffering from the passive nature of a resigned tourist capital.

Literary Florentines
Writers from Florence have had a great impact on the world. Machiavelli is widely credited with inventing modern political science and journalism, and Dante's highbrow Florentine language was so admired that it became the basis for present-day Italian. In literature Guicciardini is credited with laying the groundwork for historical prose, Petrarch for modern poetry, and Boccaccio for the prose narrative.

GEOGRAPHY AND LAYOUT

Built along the banks of the Arno, Florence is cut in two by the river, with the older part of the city lying to the north. The river has, perhaps, been a mixed blessing for the city – on the one hand supplying it with water and a transport link, but ocasionally unleashing devastating floods, as happened in 1966 *(see box on p.12)*.

Three Squares

The old historic centre might be thought of as clustering around three *piazzi*, or squares, each of which represents a different centre of influence. Piazza del Duomo surrounds the city's cathedral and is the centre of spiritual power. To the north of here lie three of the city's major churches, Santa Maria Novella (close to the decidedly secular area around the railway station), San Lorenzo and San Marco.

To the south of Piazza del Duomo is Piazza della Signoria, surrounded by *palazzi* (palaces) with medieval crenellated towers. Here is the Palazzo Vecchio (Old Palace), from where the Medici ruled over Florence. It is still the centre of temporal

power in the city, as home to the *Commune* (the city government).

To the west lies Piazza della Repubblica, the square laid out to represent a 'New Florence' during the 19th century, when the city was temporarily capital of the newly independent Italy. This might be seen as a symbol of the city's mercantile and artisan traditions. Close by are upmarket shopping streets and the main branches of the city's banks.

Across the Arno

The river not only provides a welcome sense of space after the narrow medieval streets of the old centre, it is also crossed by a number of elegant bridges, the most famous of which is the Ponte Vecchio. The views along the river are extremely beautiful, and the roads that run along its banks – popular for an evening stroll – are named after it: Lungarno (meaning 'Along the Arno').

Beyond the southern bank of the river is Oltrarno (Across the Arno), settled later than the area to the north. This was for a long time a gritty working-class district, full of workshops, but is now becoming gentrified, with trendy bars (it is also popular with students), but still remains slighty off the main tourist routes. Dominating the area, however, is the grand palace of the Medici, the Palazzo Pitti, with the beautiful Boboli Garden beyond.

Overlooking it all, from its vantage point on top of the hills, is the shrine of Florence's first martyr, the glorious church of San Miniato al Monte.

A POTTED HISTORY

Beginnings

The first settlements in and around Florence were those of the peace-loving Etruscans (from whose name we get the modern Toscana, or Tus-

Above from far left: the view from Piazzale Michelangelo; rowing on the Arno; in the Boboli Garden; historic street.

Below: picturesque Florentine rooftops.

Above from left: small is beautiful; Palazzo Pubblico; mosaic of Christ in the Baptistry; monk taking a break.

cany), who built a substantial town on the site of present-day Fiesole. They were to flourish until *c.*300BC, when the region fell to the growing power of Rome. And it was the Romans who were to found the city of Firenze (Florence) in 59BC, when they built a *colonia* for retired soldiers and named it Florentia.

The Commune

After the fall of Rome came the first glimmerings of the city-state, with the setting up of the *Commune*, and the construction of public works such as the city walls, a cathedral and the

The 1966 Flood

On 4 November 1966, after 48cm (19in) of rain had fallen in 48 hours, the River Arno burst its banks. Thirty five people were killed, 16,000 vehicles destroyed and hundreds of homes left uninhabitable as the muddy floodwaters rose to more than 6m (20ft) above street level. Heating oil was swept out of broken basement tanks. The water crashed through the museums, galleries, churches and craft shops. Thousands of works of art were damaged. The city had suffered from floods in the past – about one really serious inundation each century – but this caused more damage than any other. Student volunteers flocked to Florence from around the world to help the army, which had sent in thousands of conscripts. Restorers estimated it would take 20 years for all the damaged art objects to be restored and for Florence to recover. They were half right. Florence has definitely recovered, and many works of art are back on display, but, almost half a century on, the task of restoration is still not yet complete.

Palazzo Vecchio. However, it was with the rise of the wool trade, and then banking, from the 11th to the 13th centuries, that the city really began to assume its position of dominance.

By the 14th century Florence was the richest city in Europe, even though it often found itself at war with its neighbours, especially Siena – a rivalry that continues, albeit in a more gentle fashion, to the present day.

Renaissance Flourishing

With its wealth, and numerous skilled artisans, Florence was the ideal candidate to be the city at the heart of the Renaissance. An extraordinary concentration of artistic talent, including Giotto, Masaccio, Uccello, Brunelleschi, Leonardo, Raphael and Michelangelo, to name but a few, found work and patronage in the city, especially once the Medici took control of Florence in 1434 (a period of rule that was to last, with a few breaks, until 1737).

Foreign Rule

With the demise of the last of the Medici, Florence fell under foreign rule, first the Austrians and then the French. By this time, it was also being discovered by the British, who flocked to its art treasures as part of their 'grand tours' of the continent. Some of them came and expropriated works of art to hang in their stately homes, but others, captivated by the city, stayed and made it their home.

Unification and Independence

When ideas of nationalism began to sweep through Europe during the 19th century, Tuscany was not immune, and became a major player in the *Risorgimento* (Revival) that ended with Italian unification and independence. Indeed, for five years, from 1865 to 1870, Florence was the capital of the new state.

CONTEMPORARY FLORENCE

Since then Florence has survived Fascism under Mussolini, destruction under the Nazis, and dreadful flooding, but still remains one of the most beautiful cities in Europe with an artistic heritage unmatched almost anywhere. In many ways Florence has remained a prisoner of its original concept – namely, of a medieval Renaissance city – and finds it hard to move forward as a modern, progressive city. The sensation of being stuck in time is reinforced by the way foreign and Italian visitors, as well as Florentines, appear reluctant to consider the city in anything other than the most traditional terms. A good case in point is Japanese architect Arata Isozaki's design to build a towering, minimalist exit to the Uffizi Gallery, which has bitterly divided the city with critics dismissing it as a 'bus shelter'. The project is on ice and the stalemate has left the city hall, which sponsored the competition, in an embarrassing quandary.

A MODERN MAYOR

Although the city might appear as though preserved in aspic, it is beginning to change. Its rising star is Matteo Renzi, a young, forward-thinking man who is rejuvenating the city's flagging politics. Bucking the trend of grey-haired politicians, the progressive and energetic Renzi became president of the Florentine province at 29, and mayor of Florence at 34 – the youngest to ever hold the post. His approach is hands-on and he is determined to cut red tape, rejuvenate the city's cultural life, invest in eco-friendly transport and preserve the city's green spaces. No sooner was he elected mayor than he announced the surprise news that Piazza Duomo in the heart of the city would be banned to vehicles of any description, horses and carriages included. In 2011, Renzo called on all Italian politicians of the Berlusconi generation to retire. (The average age of Renzi's councillors is 41, and 50% are female). He is accelerating the spread of high-speed internet and WiFi in the city and posts his news on Twitter and Facebook.

Early Capitalists

For all the city's contemporary red hue, it might be argued that medieval Florentines were responsible for modern capitalism. They invented credit banking and double-entry book-keeping, as well as, in 1252, making Florence the first city to mint its own gold coin. This unit, the florin, became the currency used by merchants all over Europe.

Above: snoozing in the Tuscan sun.

Below: Matteo Renzi.

FOOD AND DRINK

Tuscan food is often basic and frugal but extremely tasty, using the freshest vegetables and best cuts of meat. Helping to wash all this down are the wonderful local Chiantis, some of the finest of Italian wines.

Above: bruschetta; blackboard favourite.

Sobriety rather than sensuality is an important element in the Florentine character, and, despite their love of food, Florentines delight in simple and robust dishes, with plenty of vegetables and plainly grilled meats, nourishing and eaten for utility as much as enjoyment. Perhaps the reason for this lies in their history. As busy people in a thriving commercial environment, they had little time for over-sophistication, and this stolid element persists to this day. Thick soups and bean stews (served in terracotta pots whatever the restaurant) and large steaks and heavy wines are typical of a meal in Florence.

MARKETS AND VEGETABLES

Olive Oil
Tuscany produces some of the world's finest olive oil, with the best of the Extra Virgin *(Extra Vergine)* ones having DOC (Denominazione D'Origine Controllata) status. From the region around Florence, look out for oils from Scansano, Seggiano and San Gimignano.

Perhaps the best introduction to the city's food is a morning spent amid the vegetable stalls of the Mercato Centrale. Here, local produce – courgettes, tomatoes, mushrooms, peppers, potatoes and aubergines – of excellent quality can be seen piled high. Florentines will happily eat any of these vegetables fried or brushed with Tuscany's purest *Extra Vergine* olive oil, and simply grilled until soft and melting.

But among these offerings, the undisputed aristocrats are the white beans or *fagioli*. Like the potato, the bean was introduced from the Americas by Florentine merchants, and it is now a staple of the city. In a soup or mixed with tuna fish, the little *fagioli* are a marvellously simple beginning to any Florentine meal. Best of all they are eaten plainly boiled with a dribbling of the new season's olive oil, thick, green and viscous, and utterly delicious.

Fresh Tuscan vegetables are rarely disappointing on their own, but together they make two of the city's great specialities, *ribollita* and *minestrone. Ribollita* means 'reboiled', leftover vegetables; these are combined to create a dense soup, which might involve any spare vegetables but should traditionally include white *cannellini* beans and *cavolo nero*, a type of black cabbage indigenous to Tuscany. The soup is then thickened with stale bread.

MEAT DISHES

Although Florence can offer a cornucopia of vegetables, in practice it is meat that is held in highest regard. For a starter try *crostini di fegato*, chicken

liver pâté on fried bread, delicious with a young white wine. Follow this with *fritto misto*, mixed meats fried in batter, or the peasant dish *stracotto*, beef stewed for several hours and especially satisfying in winter.

But, above all, Florence specialises in plain roasted and grilled meats: *arista* (roast pork), beef, lamb, especially at Easter, and even wild boar in season. Tuscany's fertile pasture produces some of the best meat in Italy, and the Florentines refuse to clutter these tastes with over-adornment. Just as simple is their treatment of chicken and pheasant.

However, the most prestigious of these – and as much a symbol of the city as the florin – is the famous *bistecca alla fiorentina* (steak Florentine). A huge, tender and succulent rib-steak from Tuscany's Chianina cattle, the *bistecca* is brushed with olive oil and charcoal-grilled over a scented wood fire of oak or olive branches, then seasoned with salt and pepper before being served, with a characteristic lack of fuss. It is quite the most delicious meat in Italy.

Another famous Florentine meat dish is *arista alla fiorentina*: roasted pork loin highly seasoned with chopped rosemary and ground pepper. The origin of this dish goes back to the 15th century. At the Ecumenical Council of 1430 in Florence, the Greek bishops were served the dish at a banquet and pronounced it *aristos*, which in Greek means 'very good'. The name stuck and became a feature of Florentine cuisine.

At the cheaper end of the culinary spectrum and in their rational desire not to waste, Florentines have even made a speciality out of tripe *(see box p.16)*. *Trippa alla fiorentina*, cooked with tomatoes and sprinkled with parmesan, is a favourite and inexpensive dish.

Above from far left: chef at Gustavino *(see p.41)*; classic pasta dish; serving up waffles; fresh anchovy starter.

Below: Tuscan pizza.

Above from left:
Tuscan desserts are
typically sophisticated;
the perfect cappucino.

Chestnuts
These nuts – *castagne*
in Italian – are a
favourite in Tuscany,
and from October
onwards you will find
them being roasted
on the city's streets.
Chestnuts are also
made into flour
and used to make
pancakes, soups
and sweet cakes.

SWEETS

If Florentine food tends to be filling,
full of flavour and simple, Florentine
dolci (desserts) make up for any lack
of complexity. In the bars, cake shops
and *gelaterie*, there is a riot of colour.
Coppe varie – bowls of mixed fruit and
water ice – compete for attention with
pastries and handmade sweets, huge
slabs of nougat, chocolate 'Florentines',
baci (the angel's kiss) and, at carnival
time, *schiacciata alla fiorentina*, a
simple, light sponge cake.

One pride of the city is the incred-
ibly rich, but delicious, *zuccotto*, a
sponge-cake mould with a filling of
almonds, hazelnuts, chocolate and
cream. There is no general agreement,
however, as to the origins of its name.
Literally translated as 'small pumpkin', *zuccotto* – being a dome-shaped
speciality – is thought by some to
refer affectionately to the Duomo, or
perhaps to be a slightly irreverent
allusion to the clergy. In the Tuscan
dialect, a cardinal's skullcap is also
called a *zuccotto*.

EATING OUT

As befits a city with so much excellent,
hearty food, there are numerous places
to eat. At the top end are the internationally renowned restaurants with
Michelin stars, reinventing Tuscan
classics for an eye-watering fee and a
wine list that would break the bank at
Monte Carlo.

These are, generally, for special occa-
sions, but due to the straightforward
nature of Tuscan cooking, you will find
excellent (perhaps even better) local
food at the rather cheaper *ristorante* and
osteria listed in this book. A *ristorante*
corresponds very closely to the UK or
US idea of a restaurant, while an *osteria*
(literally an inn) is slightly more relaxed
and, perhaps, rather rustic in feel.

In the evening, Florentines usually
eat at around 8.30pm, and the best
restaurants close relatively early – a
contrast to the late hours typical in
countries such as Spain or Portugal.

A Stomach for Offal

Some of the more unusual delicacies of Florence can be
found at its many tripe stands. Known as *tripperie*, these
small mobile stalls sell not only tripe but just about every
other part of the cow that is edible and left over after the
butcher has cut off the red meat. The offal is served up
either in a little dish with a plastic fork or on a *panino*, or
roll. The choice on offer varies, but you can usually find
most of the following dishes. *Trippa alla fiorentina* is traditionally stewed tripe with tomatoes and garlic, served
hot with parmesan; it is also served cold as a salad. *Lampredotto* are pigs' intestines, usually eaten in a roll after
having been simmered in a rich vegetable stock; *nervetti*
are the leg tendons, again cooked in stock, while *budelline*
are intestines cooked in a rich sauce. All this is normally
washed down with a glass of rough-and-ready wine, often
served in a plastic cup – there are no frills on tripe stands.
The *tripperie* are usually open all day, Mon–Sat, from about
9am to 7pm.

WINE

Perhaps the most famous of Italy's wines, Chianti is grown in seven regions surrounding Florence and Siena. Chianti is not just one wine, but many. In its seven zones, the variety of climates, producers and vineyards is staggering, ensuring a huge breadth of quality and complexity The main grape here is the Sangiovese.

The heartland of Chianti lies between Florence and Siena. This is the home of Chianti Classico, where the Chianti League was formed in the 13th century, a region that produces more consistently good wine than any other zone, except for the Rufina district. The latter, the most important wine-producing region near Florence, lies in the hills above the River Sieve. It produces some of the giants of Italian wine: Selvapiana, Castello di Nipozzano, Fatoria di Vetrie and the new heavyweight, Montesodi. The region surrounding Florence itself, the Chianti Coli Fiorentina, tends to produce wines that are heavy and coarse.

Key Names

Top labels to look for include Vino Nobile di Montepulciano, Brunello di Montalcino and Brolio – all red wines. Although the region's reds are by far the best-known and, for the most part, superior, wines in Chianti, light and simple whites are also out there. Most are based on Trebbiano and Malvasia grapes. The best white is generally considered to be the dry, elegant, but quite full-bodied Vernaccia di San Gimignano, from the town that lies west of Siena.

Vin Santo

The traditional way to end a classic Tuscan meal of Chianti and *bistecca alla fiorentina* is with *biscotti di Prato*, hard almond biscuits, dipped in a glass of dark gold Vin Santo (Holy Wine). This dessert wine is made from white Trebbiano and Malvasia grapes picked late, at 'the time of the saints' (around All Saints' Day, 1 November).

Left: Chianti, the king of Florentine wines.

SHOPPING

High-quality goods dominate shopping in Florence, especially clothing and leather wares. Some of the best Italian designers started out in the city, and their flagship stores still line Via de' Tornabuoni.

Above: designer dummy; smart suit at La Rinascente, the city's largest department store.

Markets
Florence has many fascinating street markets, selling a variety of goods. For food head for the Mercato Centrale on Piazza del Mercato, or the Mercato di Sant' Ambrogio, Piazza Ghiberti. For leather goods try the Mercato Nuovo and, especially, the Mercato di San Lorenzo.

FASHION

Alongside Milan and Rome, Florence is one of the fashion capitals of Italy. It may have an even greater claim to importance, as it was here that many of the great names of Italian fashion first opened shop. It is perhaps not surprising that many of these fashion houses first started off as makers of shoes and handbags – drawing on a long history of superb leatherwork – although almost all have now diversified to include clothing and accessories.

Designer Names

One of the most famous designers, Salvatore Ferragamo, settled in Florence in 1927 and went on to fashion shoes for the most beautiful women of the century. Still one of the most prestigious and well-known luxury brands, the historic Florence flagship store is in the Palazzo Spini Feroni (Via de' Tornabuoni 4r–14r; tel: 055-292 123; www.salvatoreferragamo.it). Fans should not miss the engaging shoe museum upstairs (charge).

The now rather flash house of Gucci (Via de' Tornabuoni 73-81r; tel: 055-264 5432; www.gucci.com) was started

in 1921 by the furrier Guccio Gucci. Until the 1950s it was a respectable, if somewhat staid, purveyor of handbags to the Florentine bourgeoisie. Once it had branched out onto the glamorous international market, it was picked up by style icons including Jackie Kennedy, and has not looked back since.

Dressing the well-heeled feet of Florentines for decades, home-grown Tod's classic loafers and bags come in all shapes, sizes and colours. The store is located at Via de' Tornabuoni 60r (tel: 055-219 423; www.tods.com).

Florence also has a strong history of fine textiles, and the Florentine house of Emilio Pucci capitalises on this with bold, brightly coloured prints that evoke the 1960s. They can be found at Via de' Tornabuoni 20-22r tel: 055-265 8082; www.emiliopucci.com).

Another great Florentine designer, Roberto Cavalli (Via de' Tornabuoni 83r; tel: 055-239 6226; www.roberto cavalli.com) is also famous for his bold prints and glamorous, sexy designs. Founded in the early 1960s, this fashion house now covers everything from children's wear to sexy evening dresses.

Vintage clothes fans should pop into Elio Ferraro, Via del Parione 47r, if

only to browse. Prices here are not for the faint-hearted.

LEATHER AND TEXTILES

Leather goods are not, of course, only available from the big-name international brands. Very high-quality bags and shoes by local artisans can be found all over the city. Other good places at the top end are Bottega Fiorentina (Borgo dei Greci 5r; tel: 055-295 411; www.bottegafiorentina.it) and Il Bisonte (Via del Parione 31-33r; tel: 055-215 722; www.ilbisonte.net). Otherwise, head for the myriad stalls of San Lorenzo market, where you can pick up cheaper, but still well-made, leather items.

Much of the wealth of the city was based on trade, especially that of textiles. It is still possible to buy exquisite fabrics in the city, and one of the best places, especially for silks, is Antico Setificio Fiorentino (Via L. Bartolini 4; tel: 055-213 861; www.setificio fiorentino.com), established in 1786. Also take a look at Casa dei Tessuti (Via de' Pecori 20-24r; tel: 055-215 961; www.casadeitessuti.com).

PAPER

Florence has been a major centre of hand-printing and bookbinding for centuries. Shops sell specialised stationery as well as frames and albums covered in handmade marbled paper.

Il Torchio (Via de' Bardi 17; tel: 055-234 2862; www.legatoriailtorchio.com) makes marbled paper to a secret recipe in its workshop, and also sells finely made leather and paper desk accessories.

Above from far left: classic designs at Dolce & Gabbana; marbled paper at Il Torchio; shop assistant at Cazature Calvani; Mary-Janes, Florence-style.

Opening Times
Traditionally shop opening times are Mon–Sat 8.30/9am–1/1.30pm and 3.30/4–7.30/ 8pm. Some places are closed on Monday morning or open only in the morning on Saturday. Department stores and other city centre shops stay open all day, and there is limited opening on Sunday. All shops usually stay open later in summer.

Left: Florence is known for its quality leather goods.

ENTERTAINMENT

With a healthy season of opera, concerts, chamber recitals and ballet, Florence puts up a good showing of the performing arts. If you just fancy a drink, however, there are also some great places for a cocktail or aperitivo.

For such a small city, Florence has an exceptional programme of internationally renowned classical musicians coming to perform, principally at the city's major festival of Maggio Musicale or as part of the Teatro della Pergola's season of chamber music. In terms of nightlife, however, the scene is fairly low-key, mostly centred around a number of chic bars in the centre of town.

MUSIC, OPERA AND DANCE

The Maggio Musicale

The Maggio Musicale festival, held from the end of April to the end of June, is the big musical event in Florence, with top names in opera, music and ballet performing in various theatres throughout the city. The main venue is the Teatro Comunale *(see p.122)*, which these days styles itself as the Teatro del Maggio Musicale Fiorentino.

Opera and Dance

The main opera and ballet season at the Teatro Comunale opens around the middle of September and runs through to Christmas. International performers

and scenographers appear regularly, particularly in operatic productions.

MaggioDanza is the resident ballet company at the Teatro Comunale, performing throughout the year; the most interesting productions are typically put on between September and December or during the Maggio Musicale festival. The Florence Dance Festival (www.florencedance.org), held in late June/early July and again in December, features well-known international and Italian names, along with up-and-coming dancers and choreographers.

Chamber Music

The principal venue for quality chamber-music concerts in Florence is the Teatro della Pergola *(see p.122)*, inaugurated in 1656 and a superb example of a 17th-century theatre. These concerts, which are run by the Amici della Musica and feature world-famous chamber groups and singers, are generally held at weekends. They are usually well publicised.

THEATRE

Florence is a great place for varied theatre, ranging from the classical

Listings

To keep up with the ever-changing scene, purchase *Firenze Spettacolo* (www.firenzespettacolo.it), the monthly listings magazine (with an English section) or the bi-weekly English magazine *The Florentine*; alternatively check the entertainment pages of *La Nazione*, the regional newspaper, or the Florence (Firenze) section of *La Repubblica*. The tourist information office at Via Cavour 1r (www.firenzeturismo.it) offers free 'What's On' brochures and publishes a daily list of musical events.

season at Teatro della Pergola to contemporary and fringe productions at tiny venues. Most productions are in Italian but the Teatro Puccini *(see p.122)* is worth a visit for its Fascist-era architecture.

CINEMA

Most foreign films shown in Florence are dubbed into Italian, but there are a few cinemas that show original versions, including the Odeon *(see p. 123)* and the occasional film festival that will use subtitles rather than dubbing. There are some open-air screenings in summer.

NIGHTLIFE

Italians enjoy going out and Florence has numerous bars, including atmospheric *enoteche* (wine bars) where you can sample regional wines by the glass.

The preprandial *aperitivo* has become a way of life. The price of a cocktail may seem steep but often a whole buffet is included in the price, providing a cheap alternative to dining in a restaurant.

Nightclubs are not as popular and tend to be located out of town, although in summer more open up to cater for tourists and foreign students. There are a number of English, Irish and Scottish pubs in the city, often showing Sky Sports.

The pedestrian heart of the city, with its floodlit buildings, is ideal for *la passeggiata*, the Italian custom of taking a stroll in the evening. Piazza della Repubblica, with its historic cafés and street musicians, is a hive of activity; other lively spots are Piazza Santa Croce and, on the other side of the river, Piazza Santo Spirito. Ponte Vecchio, with its river views, is a romantic spot to end the day.

Above from far left: Florence by night; cocktails at Colle Bereto Cafè.

Alternative Venues Outside the main festival season, many concerts are held throughout the summer in cloisters, squares, churches and even in the Boboli Garden. Usually well advertised, these concerts may be of varying standard, but the settings are often highly evocative.

Below: Teatro Goldoni's interior.

HISTORY: KEY DATES

Florence has seen more than its fair share of history, from the Etruscans to the Renaissance and conflicts between the Pope and the Holy Roman Emperor, to the Risorgimento that brought modern Italy into being.

BEGINNINGS

4th C BC	Fiesole is well-established as a powerful Etruscan city.
351BC	Etruria is conquered by the Romans.
59BC	Foundation of the Roman colony of Florentia.
AD250	The martyrdom of St Minias, to whom a shrine is dedicated on what is now the site of San Miniato church. This is the first evidence of Christianity in Florence.
4th C	Building of Santa Reparata, the city's first cathedral.
1125	Florence conquers and destroys neighbouring Fiesole.
13th C	Embroiled in factional conflicts, Florence sides with the Guelf (pro-pope) party against Ghibelline (pro-emperor) cities, such as Pisa and Siena.
1260	Siena defeats Florence at the battle of Montaperti, but is dissuaded from destroying the city.
1302	Dante, a victim of the Guelf conflict, is expelled from Florence *(see margin, left)* and begins to write *The Divine Comedy*.
1322	Completion of the Palazzo Vecchio.
1348	The Black Death kills three-fifths of the Florentine population over the next 50 years. This inspires Boccaccio to write his *Decameron*.
1384	The Florentines capture Arezzo.

THE RENAISSANCE

1400–1	A competition is held to design new doors for the Baptistry; this is regarded as the start of the *rinascita* (rebirth) or Renaissance.
1406	Florence conquers Pisa and gains a sea port.
1434	Cosimo de' Medici turns the city into an artistic and intellectual centre.
1469	Cosimo's grandson Lorenzo de' Medici assumes power.
1494	Savonarola declares Florence a republic ruled only by God.
1498	Execution of Savonarola.

Exile and Pardon
Probably Florence's greatest writer, Dante Aligheri (c. 1265–1321), was a supporter of the Guelfi Bianci (White Guelfs), who demanded more freedom from Rome. They were defeated by the Guelfi Neri (Black Guelfs) in 1301, and Dante, who was in Rome at the time, found himself in exile. In 1302, after refusing to pay a fine, he was sentenced to death by burning if he returned to Florence. This order was finally lifted in 2008, when the city's Commune (government) passed a motion to revoke the sentence.

1512	Florence is defeated by an invading Spanish army, which facilitates the return of the Medici.
1527	Florence expels the Medici again, and reverts to a republic.
1530	Pope Clement VII and Emperor Charles V besiege Florence.
1531	Florence falls.
1555	Start of Cosimo I's campaign to reunite Tuscany by force.
1570	Cosimo I is appointed Grand Duke of Tuscany.
1610	Cosimo II appoints Galileo as court mathematician.
1631	Galileo is excommunicated.

FOREIGN RULE AND INDEPENDENCE

1737	The last Medici grand duke dies without an heir and the title passes to the Austrian House of Lorraine.
1808	France annexes Tuscany.
1848	Tuscany is a vanguard in the first Italian War of Independence.
1865	Florence becomes the temporary capital of the emerging united Italy.
1919	Benito Mussolini founds the Italian Fascist Party.
1939–45	During World War II, the Nazis destroy parts of central Florence. The Ponte Vecchio is the only old bridge to survive the war.
1946	Italy becomes a republic.
1966	Florence is flooded by the River Arno and many works of art are lost.
1988	Florentines vote to exclude traffic and to control air pollution.
1993	A Mafia bomb kills five people and damages the Uffizi gallery.

Nuovi Uffizi

The Nuovi Uffizi project is a major ongoing scheme to renovate the gallery's buildings and open up more exhibition space. Partially built, the ultra-modern, seven-storey steel, stone and poly-carbonate loggia design for the gallery exit, by Japanese architect Arata Isozaki, is highly controversial among traditionalists. Conceived to relieve the bottleneck exit, it was slated by Italy's Minister of Culture and is currently on ice.

THE 21ST CENTURY

2000	The Nuovi Uffizi restoration project *(see margin, right)* is announced.
2002	The euro replaces the lira as the unit of currency in Italy.
2002–3	Michelangelo's *David* is restored.
2007	The Nuovi Uffizi renovation finally gets under way.
2008	Silvio Berlusconi returns to power for a third term.
2010	Opening of Line 1 of the long-awaited Tramvia (tram line).
2011	For the 500th anniversary of his birth, Vasari's restored home opens.
2012	New Prime Minister Mario Monti's €30 billion austerity package faces strong opposition. After a 32-year restoration Ghiberti's 'Gate of Paradise' (Baptistery doors) are unveiled. Work begins on Norman Foster's TAV railway station as part of the new high-speed rail network.

WALKS AND TOURS

PIAZZA DEL DUOMO

At the heart of this impressive square is one of the largest cathedrals in the world. Notable for both its art and architecture, the Duomo and the museum associated with it give a fine introduction to the city.

DISTANCE 1km (½ mile)
TIME A half day
START Piazza del Duomo
END Museo dell'Opera del Duomo
POINTS TO NOTE
It may be best to avoid doing this route on a Sunday, when the opening hours for both the Duomo and Museo dell'Opera del Duomo are restricted.

In peak season expect lengthy queues for the Duomo, dome and bell tower *(see margin, left)*.

The grandest monument in Florence is undoubtedly the great dome of Brunelleschi's cathedral. Along with the bell tower designed by Giotto, it dominates the city skyline and, like Michelangelo's sculpture of David, is considered to be a symbol of the city. The square in which it sits is also home to the cathedral's Baptistry, whose doors are some of the greatest achievements of early Renaissance sculpture. The spectacle of the Duomo, Campanile and Baptistry, particularly with the recent pedestrianisation of the piazza, never fails to impress.

Above: Duomo detail; top of the great dome.

Artfast Cards
Priority Artfast cards (€7, not including admission fees), enable you to skip the queues at the Duomo, dome and bell tower. They are valid for a year and available at major hotels in the city or at www.artfast.it.

PIAZZA DEL DUOMO

The walk starts at the western end of **Piazza del Duomo**, where it adjoins Piazza di San Giovanni. The best place for kick-starting your day with a strong black espresso and perhaps a small cake or savoury snack is at one of the cafés located on the two squares. Most have seats outside that offer good views of the majestic cathedral dome and the adjoining bell tower. Two good options are **Scudieri**, see ①①, and **Bar Sergio**, see ①②. From here you can get a sense of the huge scale of the cathedral, once the largest church in Christendom, and still the fourth biggest in the world (after St Peter's in Rome, St Paul's in London and the cathedral in Milan, also called the Duomo).

From either of these cafés, walk round to the front of the cathedral and join the queue outside the left-hand door to get in.

THE DUOMO

The Cattedrale di Santa Maria del Fiore is most commonly known as **Il Duomo ❶** (tel: 055-230 2885; www. operaduomo.firenze.it; Mon–Wed and Fri 10am–5pm, Thur 10am–4.30pm, Sat 10am–4.45pm, Sun 1.30–4.45pm; free), which comes from the Latin *Domus Dei*, meaning House of God. It was built as a place of worship but, just as importantly, it symbolised the ambition and pride of the city at a time when it led the world in art, science and philosophy. The cathedral took almost 150 years to build (from 1294 to 1436), but the neo-Gothic façade, the exuberance of which contrasts with the sober restraint of the buildings surrounding the square, was not added until the 19th century.

The cathedral's soaring central dome was built by Filippo Brunelleschi (1377–1446), the greatest architect and engineer of his day. As a tribute to Brunelleschi, no other edifice in Florence has been built as high as the dome since its completion in 1436, when the cathedral was consecrated by Pope Eugenius IV.

Food and Drink

① SCUDIERI
Piazza di San Giovanni 19r; tel: 055-210 733; daily 8am–8pm; €€
A long-standing and rather grand café situated close to the Baptistry and perfect for a – rather expensive – breakfast or snack. The chocolate-based patisserie is excellent, and the prices are worth it for the location and surroundings.

② BAR SERGIO
Piazza del Duomo 59r; tel: 055-214 435; daily, kitchen open from 11am; €
Opposite the Duomo is this small, somewhat cheaper, café that is a convenient place to pause before tackling the monuments. The coffee here is particularly good.

Cathedral Façade
The original façade for the Duomo was designed by Arnolfo di Cambio (d.1302), who had worked with Niccolò Pisano on the pulpit for Siena Cathedral. It took the historicising trend of the late 19th century to actually complete the job with a neo-Romanesque design by Emilio de Fabris.

The Crypt of Santa Reparata

Inside, the steps to the right lead down to the crypt (closed Sun, last entry 30 mins before closing; charge). Here, you will find Brunelleschi's simple grave: the inscription on the tomb slab compares him to Icarus, the mythical hero who learned to fly but then plunged to his death when he flew too close to the sun and it melted his wings. Brunelleschi's is the only tomb in the cathedral (although there are various memorials); his burial within its walls was a singular honour granted in recognition of his genius in building the dome. The rest of the crypt contains the ancient ruins of Santa Reparata, the church which was demolished to make way for the Duomo.

Notable Artworks

Turn left out of the crypt and right along the cathedral's north wall. You will pass a fresco of Sir John Hawkwood on horseback, painted by Paolo Uccello in 1436. Hawkwood was an English *condottiere* (mercenary), whose hired soldiers often fought for Florence. Other cities honoured military heroes with equestrian statues in stone or bronze; the fact that Hawkwood was commemorated only in a fresco is often cited as an example of Florentine miserliness.

Below: the Duomo is one of architect Brunelleschi's great masterpieces.

Nearby, you will also see a painting of Dante outside the walls of Florence, symbolising his exile *(see p.22)*. The picture was commissioned in 1465 to commemorate the bicentenary of the poet's birth. Ahead lies the sanctuary, with its lovely (mainly 15th-century) stained-glass windows. Soaring high above is the restored fresco of the *Last Judgement* painted by Vasari *(see p.37)* in 1572–9 on the underside of the dome. Vasari intended these scenes to rival the work of Michelangelo in the Sistine Chapel in Rome, but the cartoon-like scenes of devils dragging their victims to hell by the testicles do not quite match Michelangelo's more profound vision of eternal damnation.

Climbing the Dome

For a closer look at these vast and impressive figures, you can climb up to the dome (Sun–Fri 8.30am–7pm, Sat 8.30am–5.40pm, last entry 40 mins before closing; charge). To do so, exit the cathedral and circle round to the right to the Porta della Mandoria on the north side, from where you can then make the ascent.

You need stamina to tackle the 463 spiralling steps to the top of the dome, but you will be rewarded by intimate glimpses of its construction on the way up, and a fabulous view of the city once you reach the top. Climbers descending the stairs frequently pass encouraging remarks to those still arduously toiling upwards.

Before Brunelleschi, nobody had built such a huge dome since Roman times; he visited Rome to study the 2nd-century AD Pantheon in order to reinvent the ancient technique of building upwards in decreasing circles of interlocking brick. On the way up you pass between the dome's two shells. The inner one of brick, laid in a herringbone fashion, is virtually self-supporting and provided a platform for the scaffolding on which the outer shell was constructed.

The Campanile

If you have walked to the top of the dome, you may not have the inclination to also climb the 414 steps of the **Campanile di Giotto** ❷ (daily 8.30am–7.30pm, last entry 40 mins before closing; charge, combined ticket with the Baptistry), on the right as you leave the cathedral. The bell tower, was designed by Giotto in 1331, six years before his death, but only completed in 1359. The view from the top, however, is just as spectacular as that from the dome.

THE BAPTISTRY

If you decide to give the Campanile a miss, now walk over to the little octagonal **Battistero** ❸ (tel: 055-230 2885; www.operaduomo.firenze.it; Mon–Sat noon–7pm, Sun 8.30am–2pm; charge) to the west of the cathedral. Florentines have always exaggerated the

The Duomo's Dome

The external gallery that partially runs around the bottom of one section of the dome was designed by Baccio d'Agnolo in around 1506. It was originally intended to pass all the way around but work on the gallery ceased in 1515, when Michelangelo referred to it disparagingly as a 'cricket's cage'.

Loggia del Bigallo
On the southern side of the piazza, opposite the Baptistry, is the Loggia del Bigallo. This was built between 1352 and 1358, and features some fine International Gothic decoration. It now contains a small museum (Wed–Mon 10am–6pm; charge), showcasing a number of artworks.

antiquity of the Baptistry. Evidence suggests that it was built in the 6th or 7th century using Roman masonry. In the 12th century it was taken under the wing of the Calimala, the guild of wool importers, who paid for its marble cladding of green geometric designs on a white background, an innovative design admired and imitated elsewhere in Tuscany (the Duomo also follows its example).

Baptistry Doors
Set into this 10th-century building, one of the city's oldest, are three sets of bronze doors (all casts of the originals).

Those to the south were made in the 1330s by the Pisan artist Andrea Pisano and illustrate the Life of St John the Baptist, the patron saint of Florence. Although they are early works, the dynamism in the dramatic grouping of figures, and the fluency and immediacy of his style contrast with the static spirituality of 13th- and 14th-century Gothic art. Pisano was several decades ahead of his time.

Perhaps even more important are the later sets of doors by Lorenzo Ghiberti *(see box below)* that illustrate Old Testament scenes (the originals, completed in 1452, are displayed in the Museo

Ghiberti's Doors

The Renaissance proper is conventionally dated to 1401, when a competition was held to select an artist for the remaining two sets of doors. Of the seven artists who applied, the winner, Lorenzo Ghiberti (1378–1455), first made the doors for the north entrance that illustrate New Testament scenes (1424). He then made the superb 'Gate of Paradise' (Porta del Paradiso) for the east entrance, so called because Michelangelo declared they were fitting enough for the entrance to heaven. If anything, however, it was Brunelleschi's losing submission that truly indicated that the Renaissance had arrived: his trial piece was more logical in layout and, in its depiction of the actors in the drama, less idealised and more concerned with the human drama of the story than those of Ghiberti. It depicts Abraham raising the knife to Isaac's head and, just in time, the angel grasps Abraham's wrist and points to the sheep now in his view. The original bronze panel can now be seen in the Bargello *(see p.46)*.

dell'Opera del Duomo, *see below*). The door frames, which are original, contain portrait busts of 24 leading Renaissance artists; Ghiberti himself is the bald-headed figure, third up from the bottom in the centre of the doors.

The Interior

Inside the Baptistry, the ceiling is covered in striking mosaics that depict the main events of the Old and New Testaments. Executed in sparkling gold, ruby and turquoise glass cubes, they are the work of various 13th-century artists. Beneath the dome are the remains of the pavement of 1209, inlaid with the signs of the Zodiac. Two Roman columns have been incorporated into the graceful marble cladding of the walls to the right of the altar, where they flank the beautiful marble tomb of Pope John XXIII, with its bronze effigy of the sleeping pope by Donatello (1425). The Pope died on a visit to Florence in 1419.

By this time you may feel in need of a little refreshment before carrying on. One option is to try the fabulous ice-creams at **Grom**, see ③, or, for something more substantial, visit the nearby **Fiaschetteria Nuvoli**, see ④.

MUSEO DELL'OPERA DEL DUOMO

Now walk back to the Duomo and carry on around its northern side, towards the eastern end of the Piazza del Duomo. At the far end of the square is the **Museo dell'Opera del Duomo** ❹ (Museum of the Cathedral's Artefacts; tel: 055-230 2885; www.operaduomo.firenze.it; Mon–Sat 9am–7.30pm, Sun 9am–1.45pm; charge). The museum is located within a building erected by Brunelleschi in 1432 as the base from which he supervised the construction of the great cathedral dome. Today, it houses a number of outstanding works of sculpture from the cathedral and the campanile, many of which have been brought indoors to protect them from atmospheric pollution and weathering.

Above from far left: the Baptistry's magnificent bronze doors; mosaics in the dome at the Baptistry.

Food and Drink

③ GROM

Via del Campanile; tel: 055-216 158; daily, summer: 10.30am–midnight, winter: 10.30am–11pm; €
This chain of artisan *gelaterie* started in Turin and has quickly become a favourite in Florence. Located to the south of the bell tower, on the corner of Via delle Oche, Grom's ice cream contains only fresh and in-season organic fruit, with no colourings. Mineral water is used as a base for sorbets, and high-quality whole milk and organic eggs for the creams. Check out the monthly flavours and suggested pairings. Also worth trying is the almond granita.

④ FIASCHETTERIA NUVOLI

Piazza dell'Olio 15r; tel: 055-239 6616; Mon–Sat 7am–9pm; €
Situated just behind the Baptistry, this tiny eatery serves up Florentine specialities daily. Enjoy a sandwich and sip a glass of wine on the stools out front, or head downstairs, where you will find rustic seating and friendly Tuscan waiters. A much-needed inexpensive option in an otherwise overpriced area, it is very popular, and you might consider reserving ahead.

The Ground Floor

In the first two rooms, you will see Etruscan and Roman funerary urns – finds from the excavation that took place in the area between the cathedral and the Baptistry in 1971 and 1972. There are also Gothic sculptures that stood above the Baptistry doors, before they were replaced by the present-day Renaissance sculptures.

The next two rooms showcase the sculptures that Arnolfo di Cambio and his assistants carved to adorn the façade and side walls of the Duomo. These statues formed part of the half-completed 13th-century façade that was finally taken down in 1587.

To assemble this great collection of weatherworn Gothic saints and Madonnas, the museum curators scoured private collections all over Europe and museums in Berlin and Rome. Some were found in Florentine gardens and others had long been hidden, unrecognised, in the Opera del Duomo store rooms.

Further on is the Lapidarium, an assemblage of all kinds of carved and inlaid stones, some of which are now recognised as having come from the huge Romanesque baptismal font that filled the centre of the Baptistry until it was dismantled in 1577.

Above: angelic statue and bird's-eye view in the Museo dell'Opera del Duomo.

The Courtyard

Next comes the courtyard – open to the skies, until the glass roof was added as part of the recent modernisation of the museum – which originally served as a working mason's yard. It was here that Michelangelo carved his *David* – originally intended for display in front of the cathedral. Now the courtyard makes a fitting home for the original 10 panels from the Baptistry 'Gate of Paradise' *(see box p.30)*. Now that all have been restored, they can been seen in their entirety for the first time in over 30 years.

The Mezzanine

The mezzanine floor is devoted to one single work of art, Michelangelo's *Pietà*, begun in around 1550 and originally intended to adorn his own tomb. The tall, hooded figure at the centre of the group is a self-portrait; Michelangelo cast himself as Nicodemus, the rich man who donated his tomb for the burial of Christ. The rather stiff figure of Mary Magdalene, to the left, was carved by one of Michelangelo's

Food and Drink 🍽

⑤ I VISACCI

Borgo degli Albizi 80r; tel: 055-200 1956; Mon–Sat 9am–3am; €

A colourful café that serves drinks and light lunches and offers more than pasta, pizza or *panini*: choose from the *crostini*, salads or fish- or meat-based plates. Very relaxed ambience and friendly staff. Particularly good for a pre-prandial cocktail, and, later on, a DJ livens the bar up.

pupils. Dissatisfied with his work, the great master broke up the *Pietà*; it survived only because a servant kept the pieces.

The First Floor

On the first floor of the museum there are two fine *cantorie* (choir galleries), carved in marble. They were removed from the cathedral during the 17th century. Both depict young musicians in a frenzy of dancing and music-making. They were made by two of the leading artists of the day, Donatello and Luca della Robbia, between 1431 and 1438. Here, too, you will find Donatello's powerful *Mary Magdalene*, a figure of penitence carved in wood.

Beyond, a room is devoted to the panels that once adorned the base of Giotto's campanile, some made by Giotto, but the majority by Andrea Pisano. They show the *Creation of Adam and Eve* as well as the arts and sciences.

The final section of the museum is concerned with Brunelleschi's achievement in building the dome. Tools, brick moulds, pulleys and scaffolding are used to recreate the appearance of a 15th-century building site. You can also see models and drawings produced over several centuries for the cathedral façade. After years of rivalry and contention, a design was finally chosen, that of Emilio de Fabris. The façade was added in the 1880s, almost 600 years after the building was begun.

If you began your tour around lunchtime, it may well be time for an *aperitivo*. A short walk to the south of the museum on Borgo degli Albizi is a great bar, **I Visacci**, see ⑪⑤.

Above from far left: entrance to the Museo dell'Opera del Duomo; museum interior.

Donatello's Workshop

Around the corner from where Michelangelo carved his *David* (now part of the Museo dell'Opera del Duomo), was where another great Renaissance sculptor, Donatello (1386–1466), had his workshop. Almost next door to the museum, look for the building, which is now occupied by a restaurant named after the artist.

Left: taking a break in the Museo dell' Opera del Duomo.

2

ORSANMICHELE TO THE PONTE VECCHIO

The impressive space of Piazza della Signoria is arguably the heart of the city. Witness to many upheavals throughout history, it is overlooked by the towering Palazzo Vecchio, formerly the ancestral home of the Medici.

Above: Palazzo Vecchio lion; along the Arno.

DISTANCE 1km (½ mile)
TIME A half day
START Orsanmichele
END Ponte Vecchio
POINTS TO NOTE
If you are in a hurry to pack in the sights, it is possible to link this route with tour no. 3 of the Uffizi Gallery. However, this would make for a very long day of sightseeing and possible art fatigue. On its own, this walk works well as an afternoon tour.

Food and Drink 🍴
① RISTORANTE PAOLI
Via dei Tavolini 12r; tel: 055-216 215; Wed–Mon noon–3pm, 7pm–midnight; €€
This historic restaurant, founded in 1824, is a good place to try traditional Tuscan cooking. The building dates back to the 14th century, but the attractive neo-Gothic interior is actually from the early 20th century. If you are popping in for lunch, then the salads are well worth a try.

Hot Air
Politicians have addressed the public from the front of the Palazzo Vecchio since the 14th century. Originally, this was done from the raised platform, the *ringheria* (which gave rise to the term 'to harangue'), until it was demolished in 1812.

This route explores the area around the political centre of medieval Florence, the expansive Piazza della Signoria. This is the location of Michelangelo's iconic *David*, as well as the Palazzo Vecchio, once the home of the Medici rulers and now the city's town hall.

If you want to grab some lunch first, head for **Ristorante Paoli**, see 🍴①, on Via dei Tavolini, just opposite where the tour begins outside Orsanmichele.

ORSANMICHELE

Start your walk in Via de'Calzaiuoli outside the church of **Orsanmichele** ❶ (tel: 055-284 944; daily 10am-5pm, closed Mon in Aug).

Orsanmichele was built in 1337 on the site of the garden *(hortus)* of the monastery church of San Michele, and the combination of the two words gives its present name. Originally it served as an open-arcaded grain market but in 1380 the arcades were filled in and the ground floor converted to a church, while the upper storey became an emergency grain store to be used in times of siege or famine. This is a small museum

(open Monday only, charge) housing original statuary from the church.

Walk round the church, to the right, and down Via Orsanmichele, where you can study the statues in the wall niches. Each of these niches belonged to one of the city's powerful guilds, who commissioned artists to portray their patron saints. The most famous statue, Donatello's *St George*, is now replaced by a copy; the original can be seen in the Bargello *(see p. 46)*.

The Interior

At the back of the church, an aerial corridor links Orsanmichele to the 13th-century **Palazzo del'Arte della Lana** (Wool Guild Palace). The entrance to the church is located just beneath the corridor.

The centrepiece of this astonishingly rich Gothic church is Andrea Orcagna's elaborate tabernacle (1459), which is decorated with scenes from the *Life of the Virgin*, and encloses Bernardo Daddi's painting of the *Madonna* (1347). Turn left out of the church, left again in Via de' Lamberti, passing Donatello's statue of *St Mark* in the first niche, then right in Via de' Calzaiuoli, to **Piazza della Signoria ❷**.

PIAZZA DELLA SIGNORIA

This handsome square was long a place of political strife. The land and

Above from far left: Palazzo Vecchio; Orsanmichele detail; strolling outside the church; imposing Orsanmichele tower.

Below left: Palazzo Vecchio statue.

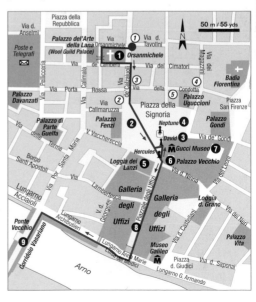

Mystery Man
To the right of the Palazzo Vecchio's main entrance, just behind the statue of Hercules, is the profile of a man scratched into the stone. It is attributed to Michelangelo.

buildings were owned by the Uberti, supporters of the Ghibelline (imperial) faction, losers to the Guelf (papal) party in the struggles that tore Florence apart in the 13th century. The property of the exiled Uberti was first left to crumble as a sign of the family's defeat, but then chosen as the site of a new palace to house the city government.

Towering over everything is the battlemented façade and campanile of the Palazzo Vecchio, which was built to house the government between 1299 and 1322. It dwarfs even the huge heroic figure of *David* ❸ (a copy – Michelangelo's original is in the Accademia, *see p.58*), Bandinelli's rather lumpy figure of *Hercules* (1534) and the licentious nymphs of Ammanati's *Fontana di Nettuno* ❹ (Neptune Fountain; 1575). These works of art,

all fronting the palace, symbolise Florence in various ways: for example, David representing a figure of defiance against tyranny; Hercules, the mythical founder of the city; and Neptune being a metaphor for the city's naval fleet, created by Cosimo I.

The Loggia of the Lancers

To the right of the Palazzo Vecchio, sheltering under the **Loggia dei Lanzi** ❺ (named after Cosimo I's bodyguard, the lancers), are several celebrated statues, including Cellini's *Perseus* grasping the severed head of Medusa, and Giambologna's renowned *Rape of the Sabine Women* (1583).

Before entering the Palazzo Vecchio you might like to take some refreshment. One option, on the square itself, is the classy **Rivoire**, see ⑪②, with its ice cream, pastries and views of the historic buildings. More low-key but still extremely attractive is the **Caffè Italiano**, see ⑪③, just to the north of the square on Via della Condotta.

PALAZZO VECCHIO

Climb the steps of the **Palazzo Vecchio** ❻ (tel: 055-276 8325; www.museicivicifiorentini.it; Fri–Wed 9am–7pm, until midnight Aug and Sept; Thur 9am–2pm; charge). The palace, now partly the town hall and partly a museum, was completely remodelled when Cosimo moved into it in 1540, having quashed republicanism in Flo-

---

Food and Drink 🍴

② RIVOIRE
Piazza della Signoria 4r; tel: 055-214 412; Tue–Sun 8am–midnight; €€
A grand café located on the *piazza*, which is famed for its handmade chocolates and drinking chocolates. Treat yourself to a coffee or *gelato* during the day or a cocktail in the early evening. While it is more expensive than other places, the outside tables offer great views over the square.

③ CAFFÈ ITALIANO
Via della Condotta 56r; tel: 055-291 082; Mon–Sat 8am–8pm; €
Decked out in wood, this old-fashioned café offers a range of beverages and light lunches such as pastas and salads. Relax with a newspaper or a book over the decent coffee or one of their speciality hot chocolates.

rence and established himself as an hereditary duke.

You enter via a *cortile* (courtyard), designed in 1453 by Michelozzo Michelozzi. The little fountain in the centre *(pictured below)* was designed by Giorgio Vasari, court architect from 1555–74, who also produced the frescoes and stucco in the surrounding arcade.

On the walls are views of Austrian cities, painted to make Joanna of Austria feel at home when she married Francesco de' Medici (Cosimo's son) in 1565. The ceiling is covered in grotesque figures in imitation of the ancient Roman paintings in the grotto of Nero's garden in Rome. Next to the ticket office, the new Tracce di Firenze (Traces of Florence) exhibition presents a pictorial history of the city, from the Middle Ages to the 20th century.

Room of the Five Hundred

The state chambers start on the first floor with the Salone dei Cinquecento (Room of the Five Hundred). This was designed in 1495 for the 500-strong ruling assembly – the Consiglio Maggiore – of the penultimate republic. It was the largest room of its time. Despite its appalling acoustics, the vast space is now used occasionally as a concert hall.

Leonardo da Vinci and Michelangelo were both commissioned to paint the walls and ceilings of the Salone dei Cinquecento, but neither got much further than experimental sketches. It was left to Vasari to undertake the work, which was executed with great speed between 1563 and 1565. Nominally, the paintings celebrate the foundation of Florence and the recent victories over its rivals, Pisa and Siena. The ubiquitous presence of Cosimo I in all the scenes, however, makes it simply a vast exercise in ducal propaganda.

It is not unusual for visitors to feel uneasy and wonder why Vasari stooped to such overt flattery. Michelangelo's *The Genius of Victory* is equally disturbing. Brutally realistic, it depicts an old man who has been forced to the ground by the superior strength of a

Above from far left: Palazzo Vecchio; *Rape of the Sabine Women* statue and lampposts in Piazza della Signoria; inside Palazzo Vecchio, former home of the Medici.

Below: fountain at the Palazzo Vecchio.

muscular youth. It was carved for the tomb of Julius II in Rome, but Michelangelo's heirs presented it to Cosimo I to commemorate the 1559 victory over Siena. The artist intended it to represent the triumph of reason over ignorance, but in this context it seems part of a gross celebration of war. Even so, artists have frequently sought to imitate Michelangelo's twisted, tortured figures, and it was one of the works most admired by the later 16th-century Mannerists.

Light relief is provided by another 16th-century work, *Hercules and Diomedes* of Vincenzo de' Rossi, a no-holds-barred tussle, in which the inverted Diomedes takes revenge by squeezing Hercules' genitals in a pain-inducing grip.

Other First-Floor Highlights

Off the main hall is the study (**Studiolo**) of the reclusive Francesco I (usually only accessible on a guided tour, *see p.39*), built between 1570 and 1575. The beautiful cupboards were used to store his treasures and the equipment for his experiments in alchemy. His parents, Cosimo I and Eleonora di Toledo, are depicted in the wall frescoes by Bronzino. Other paintings depcit the four elements.

Next in sequence comes the suite of rooms known as the Quartiere di Leone X, decorated in 1556–62 by Vasari and named after Giovanni de' Medici, son of Lorenzo the Magnificent, who was created a cardinal at the age of 13 and eventually became Pope Leo X.

Quarters of the Elements

On the floor above is the **Quartiere degli Elementi** (once again by Vasari), with allegories of the elements, including a watery scene reminiscent of the work of Botticelli. The corner room, the Terrazza di Saturno, provides fine views east to Santa Croce and south to San Miniato, while in another small room is Verrocchio's original *Boy with Dolphin* (1470).

Savonarola

Girolamo Savonarola (1452–98) was appointed as the hard-line Prior of San Marco in 1491. Under Charles VIII of France he became the leader of Florence in 1494 and ruled over the city for four years, convinced that he was an agent of God, sent to punish Florentines for their obsession with pagan philosophies, secular books and profane art. Among the draconian laws he imposed was the punishment of death for wearing 'lewd' clothes. As part of his fanatical obsession with creating a city prepared for the Apocalypse he instigated a 'bonfire of the vanities'. For this, he and his supporters collected anything they considered immoral or pagan, including a large number of works of art – among them paintings by Botticelli – and burnt them on a large pyre in Piazza della Signoria. After this, public opinion turned against him, especially when he was excommunicated and the threat of papal rule fell over the city. He was executed in 1498, and a plaque on the pavement near the Neptune Fountain marks the spot in Piazza della Signoria where he was burnt to death.

Quarters of Eleonor of Toledo

The **Quartiere di Eleonora di Toledo**, the private rooms of the beautiful wife of Cosimo I, include the chapel. A masterpiece of Florentine Mannerism, it is adorned with stunning frescoes by Bronzino (1540–5), and offers a rare opportunity to study fresco work at close quarters. The sheer range and brilliance of the colour is striking, with hues that are rarely seen in modern painting.

Eleonora's bedroom is decorated with a frieze based on her initials, and has a lovely marble washbasin; another room is painted with domestic scenes – spinning, weaving and tasks that correspond to the classical idea of virtuous motherhood. The last room shows Florentine street scenes and festivities.

Hall of Justice and Room of the Lilies

A corridor containing the serene death mask of Dante leads to the two most sumptuous rooms of the palace, the **Sala d'Udienza** and the **Sala dei Gigli**. Both have gilded and coffered ceilings, decorated with every conceivable form of ornament. The 16th-century intarsia doors between the two depict the poets Dante and Petrarch.

The Sala dei Gigli is named after the so-called lilies (irises, in reality) that cover the walls. The frescoes are by Ghirlandaio and the ceiling by the Maiano brothers. Donatello's original *Judith and Holofernes* (1460) is the highlight here, with information panels that explain how the bronze was cast and, more recently, restored.

Other Second-Floor Highlights

The **Cancelleria**, a small chamber off to the side (entered through the remains of a 13th-century window), was built in 1511 as an office for Niccolò Machiavelli during his term as government secretary. A portrait by Santi di Tito depicts the youthful, smiling author of *The Prince,* looking nothing like the demonic figure he was branded when his study of politics and pragmatism was published.

Just off the Sala dei Gigli is the **Sala Sala delle Carte**, formerly La Guardaroba (wardrobe), which contains a large 16th-century globe showing the extent of the then known world. The room is lined with wooden cupboards adorned with a remarkable series of maps.

Special Tours and the Children's Museum

The **Museo dei Ragazzi** (Children's Museum, entry in the Via de' Gondi; tel: 055-276 822; www.palazzo vecchio-familymuseum.it; Fri–Wed 9am–5pm, Thur 9am–2pm; charge) puts on a host of well-organised activities for children on a reservation-only basis. There's a Renaissance-themed playroom for three- to seven-year-olds, and actor-led workshops and tours for older children (in Italian) and parents (in English). Activities include the 'Secrets of the Palace' tours (Per-

Above from far left: crenellated Palazzo Vecchio turret; clock detail at the Palazzo Vecchio.

Poet in Residence
One famous resident of the Palazzo della Signoria – as the Palazzo Vecchio was once known – was Dante, who lived there for two months as a representative of the people.

Modern-Day Trade
The Ponte Vecchio is now a popular place for street traders. If you are after a poster of Bob Marley or want a suspect copy of a Prada handbag, you are in luck, otherwise it is more of an irritation, as traders block the road and add another obstruction to the already congested street.

Below: Ponte Vecchio reflections.

corso Segreto; daily at various times), which take in secret passages and odd corners made for the rulers, such as the Treasury of Cosimo I and the staircase of the Duke of Athens.

GUCCI MUSEO

For light relief from Medici propaganda visit the new **Gucci Museo** ❼ (Piazza Signoria; tel: 055-7592 3302; daily 10am–10pm, café and restaurant until midnight; www.gucci.com; charge) housed on three floors of the historic Palazzo della Mercanzia a stone's throw from the Palazzo Vecchio. Opened in 2011, Guccio Gucci's 90th anniversary, this is a permanent collection of Gucci exhibits which are juxtaposed with con-

temporary art installations from the collection of French magnate François Pinault. Themed rooms display a variety of Gucci gear: from zebra skin suitcases and glamorous evening gowns to a customised 1970s Cadillac and logo golf clubs, flippers and goggles. A Gucci café and restaurant, bookstore and Icon Store, where you can buy accessories and jewels designed for the museum, complete the scene.

PIAZZALE DEGLI UFFIZI AND THE PONTE VECCHIO

From Piazza delle Signoria head south to the long narrow courtyard, **Piazzale degli Uffizi** ❽, that lies between the two wings of the Uffizi Gallery, cov-

ered in full in tour no. 3. Unless you have the energy to visit the gallery at this point, continue walking down to the Arno and turn right along Lungarno Archibusieri to the **Ponte Vecchio** ❾ (literally the Old Bridge).

The oldest bridge of Florence, the Ponte Vecchio is as much a symbol of the city as the Duomo, *David*, or Palazzo Vecchio. It dates, in its present form, from 1345, replacing an earlier wooden structure that was swept away in a flood. Notably, it was the only bridge in the city to be spared being bombed during World War II; legend has it that this was because of Hitler's fond memories of it.

The Bridge's Occupants

Workshops have always flanked the Ponte Vecchio's central carriageway, and in 1565 Vasari's Corridor was built high above the pavement along the eastern side to link the Palazzo Pitti and the Palazzo Vecchio. In 1593, Ferdinando I, annoyed at the noisy and noxious trades that were carried on beneath his feet as he travelled the length of the corridor, ordered the resident butchers, tanners and blacksmiths, who threw their waste straight into the river, to be evicted.

The workshops were rebuilt and let to goldsmiths, and this traditional use has continued ever since, though no craftsmen work in the cramped but quaint premises any more. Ferdinando took the opportunity to double the rent, and so to get value for money, the gold-

smiths built the extensions overhanging the river at the back of their shops.

If, having finished the tour, you are looking for somewhere to eat, retrace your steps to Piazza della Signoria. Just off the top right-hand corner of the square is Via dei Magazzini, where you will find **Frescobaldi**, see ⑪④, with good Tuscan food, or for something a bit more modern try **Gustavino**, see ⑪⑤, on nearby Via della Condotta.

Food and Drink 🍴

④ FRESCOBALDI

Via dei Magazzini; tel: 055-284 724; Tue–Sat noon–2.30pm and 7–10.30pm; €€–€€€

Tucked away, this lovely little place dishes up flavoursome Tuscan dishes to complement its huge range of local wines. Try the *porchetta* (roast suckling pig) with a glass of Chianti from the cantina. Outside seating is available during the summer months.

⑤ GUSTAVINO

Via della Condotta 37r; tel: 055-239 9806; Mon–Fri 7–11.30pm, Sat–Sun 12.30–3pm and 7–11.30pm; €€€

This glossy restaurant's open kitchen allows you to watch your meal being prepared. The food is creative without being over-fussy, and is beautifully presented. Look out for the speciality wine-and-food evenings they run. The Canova wine bar next door is open daily (noon–11.30pm) for similar dishes but in a less formal atmosphere.

Above from far left: the bridge viewed from the north; on the Ponte Vecchio.

Above: Ponte Vecchio statue and artist/street trader.

THE UFFIZI

Quite simply, this is the world's greatest collection of Italian Renaissance art, beautifully housed in a 16th-century building that has bequeathed to us the word for an 'art gallery'.

TIME A full day
POINTS TO NOTE
To avoid huge queues book advance tickets (charge) through Firenze Musei (tel: 055-294 883; www.firenzemusei.it). The Firenze Card *(see p.100)* also enables you to skip the queues. Expect considerably higher prices when temporary exhibitions are held.

Above: book ahead to avoid the queues.

Gallery Origins
In 1580, the open loggia of the Uffizi administrative building was turned into rooms for the art collections of the Medici; effectively a *galleria* enclosed in glass. Today's expression 'art gallery' is derived from it.

A visit to the **Galleria degli Uffizi** (tel: 055-238 8651; www.polomuseale. firenze.it; Tue–Sun 8.15am–6.50pm; charge) is a memorable experience. Here are some of the most famous works of art ever made and the breadth of the Italian collections, including pieces by Giotto, Botticelli, Leonardo, Raphael and Michelangelo, is astounding.

The Uffizi is unique in that most of its paintings were created in Florence, by Florentine artists, for Florentine patrons. Many were commissioned, collected or inherited by the Medici, whose last surviving family member, Anna Maria Ludovica, bequeathed the entire collection to the citizens of Florence upon her death in 1743.

THE BUILDING

The ticket office for the gallery is located in the long, narrow courtyard of Piazzale degli Uffizi. The courtyard is always thronged with people and unless you have have booked tickets in advance, you will have to join the queue.

The Uffizi itself was built in 1560 by the court architect, Giorgio Vasari (1511–74) to provide offices *(uffici)* for the Medici administration. The building has always been used by the Medici to display prize works of art from their collections, including numerous Roman and Greek statues.

Layout
The main collection is on the second floor, with four further rooms located on the first floor and temporary exhi-

Food and Drink
① MUSEUM CAFÉ
Galleria degli Uffizi; tel: 055-238 8651; Tue–Sun 8.30am–6pm; €
The Uffizi's café is nothing extraordinary in culinary terms – dishing up coffee, cakes, sandwiches and simple meals – but it does sit on top of the Loggia dei Lanzi with a great view over Piazza della Signoria.

bitions held on the ground floor. The museum's **café**, see ⓘⓘ, is at the end of the West Corridor on the second floor.

The on-going 'Nuovi Uffizi' project (www.nuoviuffizi.it) aims to double the exhibition space currently available by opening new areas to the public. Some elements of this project have not been without controversy, especially the design for a new exit by the Japanese architect Arata Isozaki (b.1931).

THE SECOND FLOOR

Begin on the second floor, where rooms 2 to 4 are dedicated to works from Siena and Florence during the pre-Renaissance Duecento and Trecento (13th and 14th centuries). Notable pieces here include Cimabue's late 12th-century *Maestà* (or Virgin Enthroned) and his pupil Giotto's *Ognissanti Madonna*

(1310). These contrast with the more conservative works of the later International Gothic (rooms 5 and 6) although some of these are still exquisite, particularly Lorenzo Monaco's *Coronation of the Virgin Mary* (1414).

The Early Renaissance

Room 7 is dedicated to the founders and leading figures of the early Renaissance, who explored purely secular subjects for the first time in Western art since antiquity. Uccello's *Battle of San Remo* (1456) celebrates the Florentine victory over long-time rivals, the Sienese. Other artists here include Masaccio – see especially his *Madonna and Child with St Anne* (1424) – and Fra Angelico.

The Filippo Lippi Room (8) holds the Franciscan monk's lovely mid-15th-century *Madonna and Child with Two Angels*, which is notable for its

Above from far left: the Uffizi by night; the gallery backs onto the Arno.

Mafia Bomb
In 1993 the mafia exploded a car bomb outside the building, killing five people. The explosion damaged several of the gallery's rooms as well as part of the Vasarian Corridor, and the restoration took several years to complete.

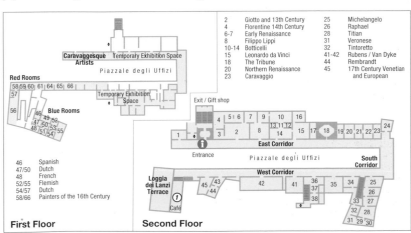

2	Giotto and 13th Century	25	Michelangelo
4	Florentine 14th Century	26	Raphael
6-7	Early Renaissance	28	Titian
8	Filippo Lippi	31	Veronese
10-14	Botticelli	32	Tintoretto
15	Leonardo da Vinci	41-42	Rubens / Van Dyke
18	The Tribune	44	Rembrandt
20	Northern Renaissance	45	17th Century Venetian
23	Caravaggio		and European

Caravaggesque Artists   Temporary Exhibition Space

Piazzale degli Uffizi

Red Rooms

58 59 60 | 61 | 64 | 65 | 66

57

Temporary Exhibition Space

56

Blue Rooms

46 49 52
47 50 53 55
48 51 54

Exit / Gift shop

4 | 5 | 6 | 7 | 9 | 10 | 16
3 | 2 | 8 | 13 11 12 | 15 | 17 | 18 | 19 20 21 22 23 | 24
1 | | | 14

East Corridor

Entrance

Piazzale degli Uffizi

South Corridor

West Corridor

46	Spanish
47/50	Dutch
48	French
52/55	Flemish
54/57	Dutch
58/66	Painters of the 16th Century

Loggia dei Lanzi Terrace

Café

45 43
44

42

41

36
37
38

35 34

25
26
27

33
32
31 29 30

28

First Floor

Second Floor

Above from left:
Titian's *Venus of Urbino*; Fiorentina's *Angel Musician*.

realistic treatment of landscape. Also here are Piero della Francesca's honest portraits of the *Duke and Duchess of Urbino I* (*c*.1465) in all their ugly glory.

The Botticelli Rooms (10 to 14) are the most popular, containing the world's best collection of work by the artist. Highlights include the mythological paintings – the *Birth of Venus* (*c*.1485) and *Primavera* (*c*.1480) – which fused ideas of the spiritual and the secular. The meaning of the latter remains a subject of ardent discussion, while the figure of Venus has overtones of the Virgin Mary.

The High Renaissance

The High Renaissance arrives with room 15. On show are early paintings by Leonardo da Vinci, including the *Annunciation* (1475) and the unfinished *Adoration of the Magi* (1482), as well as works by Perugino and Signorelli.

The Tribuna (room 18) is an octagonal room lit from above, with a mother-of-pearl-encrusted ceiling by Buontalenti. The room's structure and decor were designed to allude to the four elements. It used to exhibit the Medici's most highly prized objects; today its best-known painting is *Angel Musician* (*c*.1520) by Fiorentina.

The High Renaissance continues in room 19, which exhibits Perugino and Signorelli's work. These Umbrian artists worked during the 15th and 16th centuries, and the latter's tondo (circular painting) of the *Holy Family* is reputed to have inspired Michelangelo's version. Room 20 offers a break from Italian art, with works by the German painter Albrecht Dürer (1471–1528), including his *Madonna with the Pear* (1526), and by Cranach. The last few rooms on the Eastern Corridor hold works from the Venetian school in room 21; followed by Holbein and other Flemish and German Realists in room 22; and more Italian art by Mantegna and Correggio in room 23. Room 24 has a collection of miniatures.

Michelangelo and Raphael

The Western Corridor starts with the Michelangelo Room and his vivid *Holy Family* tondo (*c*.1506). This prelude to Mannerism was produced for the wedding of Angelo Doni to Maddalena Strozzi. Early works by Raphael – such as the glowing *Madonna of the Goldfinch* (1505–6) – and del Sarto's *Madonna*

The Vasarian Corridor

One of the most intriguing parts of the Uffizi is the Corridoio Vasariano, linking the gallery with the Palazzo Pitti on the other side of the Arno. It was built by the eponymous Vasari in 1565, so that the Medici Grand Dukes could pass between the offices at the Uffizi and their residence in the Palazzo Pitti without being seen. The passage passes over the Ponte Vecchio, through the church of Santa Felicità and on into the Pitti. The walls are hung with 17th- and 18th-century paintings and also a series of artists' self-portraits. It is only possible to visit the corridor as part of a pre-booked tour organised by private tour agencies. Contact Florence Town (tel: 055-012 3994, www.florencetown.com) for information..

of the Harpies (1515–17) can be seen in room 26. The subsequent room (27) is the last to focus on Tuscan art before moving on to other regions of Italy.

Room 28 displays work by Titian, including the erotic *Venus of Urbino* (1538). Rooms 29 and 30 focus on Emilia-Romagnan art and the Mannerists Dosso Dossi and Parmigianino. Veronese's *Annunciation* (*c*.1556) is in room 31, while Tintoretto's sensual *Leda and the Swan* hangs in room 32. A few rooms are dedicated to works of the Cinquecento (16th century), before the Flemish art of Rubens and van Dyck in room 41. The Niobe Room holds sculpture, while room 44 has works by Rembrandt.

THE FIRST FLOOR

On the first floor are five rooms of 17th-century Italian paintings as well as the Verone sull'Arno, the bottom of the U-shaped corridor, which looks over the River Arno and the Piazzale degli Uffizi on the other side.

The Caravaggio Room holds three paintings by the troubled artist, whose style is characterised by his realism and use of light (see his *Sacrifice of Isaac*, 1601–2). Caravaggio's method inspired the works by other artists contained in the same room and the next three. The last room adjacent to the Verone is the Guido Reni Room, where paintings by the 17th-century artist are displayed.

Having feasted your eyes, you are now probably ready for more solid sustenance. Two reliable places close by are **Antico Fattore**, see ⑂②, and **Buca dell'Orafo**, see ⑂③.

Stendhal Syndrome
Named after the famous 19th-century French writer, born Henri-Marie Beyle (1783–1842), who wrote of suffering from it while visiting Florence, this medical condition – characterised by dizzy spells and fainting – is said to come on after too much exposure to art. During the Romantic era it was all the rage to swoon when confronted with famous – and admittedly exquisite – works of art, though it is just as likely to be brought on by lack of sustenance as a hyper-sensitive aesthetic awareness.

Food and Drink 🍴

② ANTICO FATTORE
Via Lambertesca 1/2r; tel: 055-288 975; Mon–Sat 12.15–3pm, 7.15–10.30pm; www.anticofattore.it €€
This long-standing *trattoria* close to the Uffizi offers good meat and game dishes as well as the standard Tuscan and Florentine dishes such as *trippa* (tripe) and *ribollita* (vegetable and bread soup).

③ BUCA DELL'ORAFO
Via dei Girolami 28r; tel: 055-213 619; Tue–Sat noon–2.30pm, 7.30–9.45pm; €€
This generations-old *trattoria* is in the shadow of the Ponte Vecchio. It is tiny and crowded but has charm and good simple Tuscan fare, based on pasta and pulses.

4

THE BARGELLO
AND SANTA CROCE

This walk offers a chance to visit an outstanding collection of sculpture in the Bargello. You can also eat in a chic, modern restaurant, sample some delicious ice cream and visit the tombs of Galileo, Machiavelli and Michelangelo.

San Firenze
Giving its name to the *piazza* on which it stands, the Baroque church of San Firenze now houses the city's Tribunale, or law courts, and is often surrounded by gun-toting *carabinieri*.

Below: Piazza Santa Croce.

DISTANCE 800m (½ mile)
TIME A full day
START The Bargello
END Santa Croce
POINTS TO NOTE
Begin this tour mid-morning with a visit to the Bargello, which shuts at 1.50pm, then break for lunch, before carrying on to Badia Fiorentina. It is best to do this tour on Monday, as that is the only day the church is open to visitors (3–6pm).

Although this tour only covers a short distance it is worth taking your time over it. Between them, the museum at the Bargello and the church of Santa Croce introduce you to many of the most famous artists and thinkers – and their works – in the history of the city.

THE BARGELLO

Start your tour outside the **Bargello** ❶ (tel: 055-294 883; www.polo museale.firenze.it; daily 8.15am– 1.50pm, closed 1st, 3rd and 5th Sun and 2nd and 4th Mon of the month; charge) on the edge of Piazza San Firenze. This striking building with its tall, crenellated tower was built in 1255 as the city's town hall but was later used as a prison, as the names of the surrounding streets remind us: Via dei Malcontenti (Street of the Miserable) was the route taken from the Bargello to the gallows. The inner courtyard, where criminals were once executed, is now a peaceful spot, its walls studded with stones that are carved with heraldic arms.

The Collections

The Bargello now contains the most important collection of sculpture in Florence, and its large holdings are worth several visits. However, those with limited time will want to concentrate on its undoubted star attractions.

The courtyard is surrounded by a cloister, which contains, among other works, Giambologna's original of *Oceanus* (1570–5) from the Boboli Garden *(see p.73)*. Off to the right is the Sala Michelangelo, including one of the sculptor's first great works, the *Drunken Bacchus* (1496–7), who seems to be staggering off his pedestal.

A stately external staircase leads up to the first floor loggia where there is a lovely display of bronze birds made by Giambologna for the grotto of the Medici's Villa di Castello. On the right of the loggia is the Salone di Donatello,

where you will find two of the most important works of the Renaissance: Donatello's *St George* (1416–17), commissioned by the Guild of Armourers for their niche on the exterior of Orsanmichele; and his erotically charged, and newly restored, *David* (n.d.), who is wearing little more than an enigmatic smile. On the right-hand wall are the two trial panels made by Ghiberti and Brunelleschi, the winner and runner-up respectively in the competition of 1401 to find a designer for the Baptistry doors *(see p.30)*; both panels depict the *Sacrifice of Isaac*.

Other highlights include the Sala del Verrocchio on the second floor, which has an excellent display of Tuscan sculpture from the 15th century, and, also on the second floor, the rooms given over to the museum's large collection of bronzes. Here you will find the model

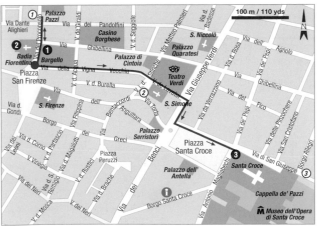

Historic Ball Game

Piazza Santa Croce has been used as a football pitch since the 16th century. A plaque on the Palazzo dell'Antella at no. 21 marks the centre line of the pitch. *Calcio storico*, a rather violent early form of football, is still played here on the feast of San Giovanni (24 June).

of Giambologna's *Rape of the Sabine Women*, which stands in the Loggia dei Lanzi on the Piazza della Signoria.

After taking in as many of the sculptures as you can manage, it will be time for lunch. A chic option for lunch is **Angels**, see ⑪①, just to the north of the Bargello on the left-hand side of Via dei Proconsolo.

BADIA FIORENTINA

After suitable refreshment walk back down Via dei Proconsolo to the **Badia Fiorentina ②**, the church opposite the Bargello on the corner of Via Dante Alighieri (tel: 055-264 402; Mon 3–6pm; free). The church of a Benedictine abbey, founded in 978, but considerably altered between 1627 and

1631, it merits a visit on account of a fine painting by Filippino Lippi, the *Apparition of the Virgin to St Bernard* (1485) just inside the door.

The church's other attraction is the **Chiostro degli Aranci** (accessed to the right of the high altar), named after the orange trees that once grew here. The lovely cloister, adorned with damaged 15th-century frescoes depicting the miracles of St Bernard by Rossellino, offers excellent views of the Badia's six-sided Romanesque bell tower.

Leaving the Badia Fiorentina follow the Via della Vigna Vecchia opposite. At the second turning to the right look for the **Gelateria Vivoli**, see ⑪②, a well-known ice cream parlour.

SANTA CROCE

Carry on to the end of Via della Vigna Vecchia and Via de'Lavatori, then turn right into Via Guiseppe Verdi down to Piazza Santa Croce fronting the church of **Santa Croce ③** (tel: 055-246 6105; www.santacroceopera.it; Mon–Sat 9.30am–5pm, Sun 2–5pm, last entry 30 mins before closing; charge, includes entrance to the Museo dell'Opera di Santa Croce and the Pazzi Chapel). This Gothic building is the burial place of many famous Florentines.

The Interior

On the right of the entrance is Michelangelo's tomb, carved by Vasari; a 19th-century monument to Dante

Galileo

Although born in Pisa, astronomer and mathematician Galileo Galilei (1564–1642) had strong ties with Florence. He first taught mathematics in the city, but after he discovered four small celestial bodies orbiting Jupiter, which he shrewdly named 'the Medicean stars', he was appointed Mathematician and Philosopher to the Grand Duke of Tuscany. He became an outspoken proponent of the Copernican system, which theorised that everything revolved around the sun. This did not sit well with the Catholic Church, which sent him into exile, first in Siena then in his villa in Arcetri, near Florence. He remained there under house arrest until his death. The city's Museo di Storia della Scienza (Science Museum) reopened in 2010 under the new name Museo Galileo (Piazza dei Giudici 1, tel: 055-265 311, www.museogalileo.it), with sections devoted to the astronomer.

(he refused to return to the city that sent him into exile and is buried in Ravenna); and the grave of the statesman Niccolò Machiavelli.

One of the most important monuments, however, is that of the humanist Leonardo Bruni, a superb piece of Renaissance design by Rossellini in 1446–7.

The famous Cappella Bardi and Cappella Peruzzi (to the right of the high altar) are covered in frescoes depicting, in the first, the *Life of St Francis*, and the second the *Life of St John the Baptist* and *St John the Divine*. These paintings by Giotto are the best of his surviving works in Florence. The frescoes of the Cappella Baroncelli were once thought to be by Giotto, but are now attributed to his talented pupil Taddeo Gaddi. The frescoes in the Cappella Maggiore, depicting *The Legend of the True Cross*, were painted by his son Agnolo Gaddi. These are undergoing restoration and are on view to visitors who were able to ascend 7 levels on guided tours for wonderful close-up views of restored frescoes. (Visits may end in 2013; for information email booking@santacroceopera.it). The corridor on the right leads past the sacristy to a chapel containing the now-empty grave of the astronomer and mathematician Galileo *(see box opposite)*. His body was moved to the north aisle in 1737.

Museo dell'Opera di Santa Croce

Adjoining the church is the Museo dell'Opera di Santa Croce (same opening times as the church), showcasing works including Cimabue's outstanding 13th-century *Crucifixion*, which had to be heavily restored after the 1966 floods. The museum has two serene cloisters leading to the Capella de' Pazzi, a noble building of white walls and *pietra serena* (grey sandstone) pilasters. Designed by Brunelleschi, it is considered to be one of the purest works of the Renaissance.

Having finished in Santa Croce, you may be approaching time for an *aperitivo* and something to eat. Just alongside the church, on Via di San Giuseppe, is **Baldovino Enoteca**, see ①③.

Above from far left: stained-glass window at Santa Croce; one of the church's celebrated frescoes.

Food and Drink

① ANGELS
Via del Proconsolo 29/31; tel: 055-239 8762; www.ristoranteangels.it; daily noon–11.30pm; €€€
A chic bar and restaurant well known for its modern Italian cooking. Try dishes such as duck with balsamic vinegar and preserved fruits, or the gnocchi filled with pumpkin. You can make dinner reservations on their website. The classy bar is open for cocktails and aperitivi from 6pm.

② GELATERIA VIVOLI
Via Isole delle Stinche 7; tel: 055-292 334; Tue–Sat 7.30am–9pm, Sun 9am–9pm; €
Although this has a reputation for being one of the best places for *gelati* in Florence there are too many flavours for each to be truly world class. The chocolate ones are pretty good, though, and it is worth a visit in the summer.

③ BALDOVINO ENOTECA
Via di San Giuseppe 22r; tel: 055-241 773; www.baldovino.com; daily 11.30am–3.30pm, 7–11pm; €–€€
This recently revamped bistro-style *trattoria*/pizzeria offers creative pastas, substantial salads, Tuscan 'fish 'n' chips, wood-fired pizzas and fine wines. Café Baldobar next door is open all day for coffee, pastries and wine.

SANTA MARIA NOVELLA TO SAN MARCO

The north of the city is home to three of Florence's most important churches: Santa Maria Novella, San Lorenzo and San Marco. They are beautiful buildings in their own right, and each is full of important works of art.

Famous Family
The Rucellai were a great Florentine family. Their name and wealth comes from *oricello*, a costly red dye from a lichen imported from the island of Mallorca.

DISTANCE 3km (2 miles)
TIME A half or a full day
START Piazza Santa Maria Novella
END Piazza San Marco
POINTS TO NOTE
It is only possible to do this tour in its entirety at weekends, as the church of San Marco closes at 1.50pm during the week. On weekdays, it is a half-day tour, and you could visit San Marco first thing as an add-on to tour 6, which begins in Piazza San Marco, prior to a visit to the Accademia (see p.58).

Food and Drink

① J.K. PLACE
Piazza Santa Maria Novella 7; tel: 055-264 5181; 11am–11pm (breakfast 7–11am); €€€€
In this plush design hotel with the atmosphere of a private house you can order a drink (the cocktails are particularly good), a coffee and light snacks or a meal from anywhere in the building including the bar. There is a lovely lounge space with a large fireplace as well as a romantic rooftop terrace. Sunday brunch is served 12.30–3pm.

Begin the tour at **Piazza Santa Maria Novella ❶**, preferably with a relaxing breakfast or a coffee in the chic design hotel J.K. Place, see ⑪①. The vast square was used for the annual chariot race *(Palio dei Cocchi)* from the 16th to the 19th centuries: the granite obelisks at each end of the green, resting on the backs of Giambologna's *Turtles* (1608), marked the turning points on the race track.

SANTA MARIA NOVELLA

Dominating Piazza Santa Maria Novella is the monumental church, after which the square is named. Its graceful façade of green-and-white marble incorporates the name of the Rucellai family *(see margin, left)* and their symbol, a billowing ship's sail, representing trade.

The family, who commissioned the architect Leon Battista Alberti (1404–72) to build the façade in 1470, formed a marriage alliance with the Medici; you will see that family's ring-and-ostrich-feather symbol among the complex geometric patterning.

The Cemetery

You enter the church of **Santa Maria Novella** ❷ (tel: 055-219 257; Mon–Thur and Sat 9am–5pm, Fri 11am–5.30pm and Sun 1–5pm, last entry 30 mins before closing; charge) through the cemetery to the right. The wall arcade surrounding the cypress-shaded grounds is carved with the coats of arms of the bankers, merchants and clothiers, whose family members are buried here.

Built in the 14th century, the cemetery is a reminder that the city was then in the grips of the Black Death. Boccaccio used the setting of this church as the springboard for his amusing *Decameron* (*c.*1344–50), in which a group of aristocrats escape to a villa outside Florence to avoid the disease. To entertain each other, they take turns to tell the 100 tales referred to in the title.

The Interior

The interior of the church is a breathtaking masterpiece of Gothic design, the soaring arches of the nave emphasised with alternating bands of white and grey stone. Hanging in the nave is Giotto's huge, emblematic *Crucifix*, dating to *c.*1290.

Another crucifixion features in Masaccio's fresco the *Trinity, Mary and St John* (1427), located in the north aisle, a landmark in the development of perspective in early Renaissance art. Behind the high altar are Ghirlandaio's colourful frescoes, the *Life of the Virgin* and *St John the Baptist* (1485–90). These repay detailed study and give a good idea of the living conditions of wealthy Florentines in the late 15th century. Equally compelling are Filippino Lippi's fres-

Above from far left: *Virgin and Child*, cloisters and Gothic church tower at Santa Maria Novella; one of Giambologna's turtles, Santa Maria Novella.

Below: the church of San Marco.

Railway Station

Santa Maria Novella railway station *(above)*, just behind the church of the same name, was the first building in Italy to be designed by Giovanni Michelucci in 1935 in the Rationalist style. The station's clean, functional lines were remarkably avant-garde for the time, but the services are insufficient for today's needs and the station is undergoing a major revamp.

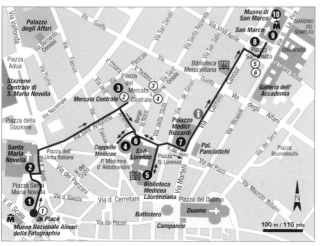

coes (1497–1502) in the Strozzi Chapel, to the right of the altar.

Lippi's theatrical style and love of the bizarre are well displayed in these scenes from the *Lives of St Philip* and *St John the Evangelist* (1502), which form the monumental setting for Benedetto da Maiano's tomb, built in 1486 for the wealthy banker Filippo Strozzi.

Museum and Cloisters

There are more notable frescoes in the church's **cloisters** which are included in a visit to the museum (Fri–Mon 9am–4pm, charge, tucked away to the left of the church facade. The **Chiostro Verde** (Green Cloister) is the most important, being the location of Uccello's dramatic *Noah and the Flood*

(1450): the cloister was so named for the predominant colour of these frescoes. Damaged by the floods of 1966, they have been leached of much of their colour, but they still remain powerful and surprisingly modern in concept: Noah's Ark is not the traditional stumpy boat, but a vast, futuristic ship. The Spanish Chapel in the Dominican monastery has a fine fresco cycle by the little-known Andrea di Buonaiuto (1365-7) representing the teachings of St Thomas Aquinas.

MERCATO CENTRALE

Leave the church and turn right onto the pedestrianised Via degli Avelli. You will soon reach Piazza dell'Unita

Below: Santa Maria Novella's cloisters.

Italiana; turn right along Via Sant' Antonino and walk down to the entrance to the huge **Mercato Centrale** ❸ (Central Market).

The stalls on the ground floor sell an abundance of meat, fish and cheese, while upstairs, under the towering glass-and-cast-iron roof, you can buy fruit, vegetables and flowers. You can also sample some Florentine specialities sold from the cooked-meat stalls or cafés downstairs; the *porchetta* (roast suckling pig) is delicious.

SAN LORENZO MARKET

We recommend you come back here for lunch, but first head south into Via dell'Ariento, where you start to pass through the huge, bustling San Lorenzo market. The stalls next to San Lorenzo church are geared to tourists and sell T-shirts, leather work and souvenirs. The deeper in you go, the more stalls you will find catering to the needs of ordinary Florentines, selling bargain-priced clothes, shoes, fabrics and table linen.

In 1990 the city administration tried to close down the market; at least, the part of it that crowds around the church. Eventually, the police gave up in the face of determined resistance from stallholders. As you walk through the market, don't neglect the little shops either side of the street, almost hidden by the stalls, where you will find all sorts of necessities for sale.

MEDICI CHAPELS

When you reach the Piazza San Lorenzo, right in front of you, and attached to the large bulk of the church of San Lorenzo *(see p.54)*, are the **Cappelle Medicee** ❹ (Medici Chapels; daily 8.15am–1.50pm, closed 1st, 3rd and 5th Mon and 2nd and 4th Sun in the month; www.polomuseale.firenze.it; charge), the entrance to which is on Piazza Madonna degli Aldobrandini just to the right.

Capella dei Principi

When you first enter the chapels you will pass through the extraordinary **Cappella dei Principi** (Chapel of the Princes), the walls of which are covered in costly, multicoloured marble. The enormous sarcophagi here commemorate the 16th- and 17th-century Grand Dukes of Tuscany.

Sagrestia Nuova

From here, a corridor leads on to the **Sagrestia Nuova** (New Sacristy); though sober in contrast to the Cappelle Medicee, it contains some stupendous sculptures. The later members of the Medici family are buried here, and it was the last – and perhaps the greatest – of all Michelangelo's works for his aristocratic patrons in Florence.

The rather modest tomb of Lorenzo de'Medici is marked by Michelangelo's unfinished *Madonna and Child*. To the left is the tomb of Lorenzo's grandson,

Lorenzo's Staircase

The staircase that dominates the Laurentian Library's entrance vestibule was built by Bartolomeo Ammannati in 1559. Michelangelo had left Florence in 1534 before work on the library was finished, leaving only a wax model of the stairs as an indication of his wishes.

also called Lorenzo (1492–1519); it is draped with the figures of Dawn and Dusk, while opposite is the tomb of Lorenzo's son, Giuliano. This features the awesome figures of Night and Day, symbolising the temporal and eternal forces of nature, and was carved between 1520 and 1533. Ironically, while working on them, Michelangelo was involved in the battle against the besieging forces of the Medici, to keep Florence as an independent republic. When that battle was lost, it is thought that Michelangelo hid from his patrons in this chapel. On the walls of a small room to the left of the altar are the charcoal sketches he made at this time.

LAURENTIAN LIBRARY

When you leave the Cappelle Medicee turn right along the side of the church and walk down to Piazza San Lorenzo. To the left of the front of the church is the entrance to the **Biblioteca Medicea Laurenziana** ❺ (Laurentian Library; tel: 055-211 590; www.bml.firenze.sbn. it; Mon–Sat 9.30am–1.30pm; charge includes entrance to church), which lies at the far end of a serene cloister, from where there are unusual views of Giotto's campanile and the Duomo.

Highlights

The library, with its extraordinary vestibule and staircase, was designed by Michelangelo from 1524. His client was the Medici pope, Clement VII,

and the library was built to house part of the famous collection of antique Greek and Latin manuscripts collected by Cosimo and Lorenzo de' Medici. Depending on what is currently on display, you may see Pliny the Younger's hand-written text, a 1436 printing of Plutarch's *Moralia* (Morals) and a Greek edition (1496) of the works of the 15th-century humanist, Poliziano, with notations.

LUNCH BREAK

Before tackling the church of San Lorenzo itself, you may be ready to get something to eat. Retrace your steps a little and head back up Via dell'Ariento to Piazza del Mercato Centrale. There are some excellent places to eat in and around the market. Among them are **Nerbone**, see ⑪②, inside the market itself, and two *trattorie* just outside, **Mario**, see ⑪③, and **Zà Zà**, see ⑪④.

SAN LORENZO

After lunch walk back down to the front of **San Lorenzo** ❻ (tel: 055-264 5184; Mon–Sat 10am–5.30pm, Mar–Oct: also Sun 1.30–5pm; charge), which you enter through a door in the unfinished façade. The interior was mainly designed by Brunelleschi and is remarkable for the elegant sobriety of the grey-and-white walls.

Just before the central domed crossing are two huge marble pulpits

carved by Donatello with scenes from the *Passion* and *Resurrection of Christ*. To the north of the pulpits, Bronzino's huge fresco of the *Martyrdom of St Lawrence* (1569), is unmissable. To the left, and often overlooked, is a more recent painting by Pietro Annigoni (1910–88) of the young Jesus with Joseph in a carpenter's workshop.

Famous Tombs

The church was once used for state funerals, and early members of the Medici family are buried here. Cosimo, who died in 1474, is buried in a vault in front of the high altar. His father, Giovanni di Bicci de'Medici (died 1429), the wealthy banker who founded the powerful dynasty, is buried in the Sagrestia Vecchia (Old Sacristy), off the north transept, built by Brunelleschi as the family mausoleum. Donatello made the bronze entrance doors (1437–43) with their animated figures of apostles, saints, martyrs and fathers of the Church. The circular tondi (1435–43) in the chapel walls depicting the *Evangelists* and the *Life of St John the Evangelist* in terracotta and plaster relief are his too.

Giovanni's sarcophagus in the centre of the chapel is by Buggiani (1434). His grandsons, Giovanni (died 1463) and Piero de'Medici (died 1469), are buried in the huge urn-like sarcophagi of porphyry and bronze set into the walls; this was designed by Verrocchio in 1472.

MEDICI-RICCARDI PALACE

Having left the church, turn right into Via de' Gori, and back into part of the bustling San Lorenzo street market. Turn left down Via Camillo Cavour, past the Tourist Office at no. 1r, and you reach the entrance to the **Palazzo Medici-Riccardi** ❼ (tel: 055-276 0340; www.palazzo-medici.it; Thur–Tue 9am–7pm; last admission 6.30pm; entrance limited to 10 visitors every 7 minutes so be prepared to queue; charge). This rather grim (and deliberately unostentatious) palace was built for Cosimo de'Medici between 1444 and 1464. It was from here that Cosimo and his heirs operated as

Above from far left: exterior of San Lorenzo; fresco in San Lorenzo.

False Start

In 1516, Pope Leo X commissioned Michelangelo to design San Lorenzo's façade. Michelangelo visited Carrara to select marble for the work, but the Pope then changed his mind and asked the artist to turn his attention to the Sagrestia Nuova instead.

Food and Drink 🍴

② NERBONE
Piazza del Mercato Centrale, inside the market; tel: 055-219 949; Mon–Sat noon–3pm; €
One of the most popular lunch spots of the area, Nerbone serves up local dishes, such as *tripa alla fiorentina* (tripe in a tomato sauce), with seasonal ingredients on a daily menu. The *panino con bollito* (boiled beef sandwich) is a favourite.

③ MARIO
Via Rosina 2r; tel: 055-218 550; Mon–Sat noon–3pm; €
Hidden away behind market stalls, this *trattoria* boasts a lively atmosphere and is popular with the local stallholders. Try the typical *ribollita* (vegetable and bread soup).

④ ZÀ ZÀ
Piazza del Mercato Centrale 26r; tel: 055-215 411; daily noon–3pm, 7pm–1am; €€–€€€
Set in the piazza behind the market, this lively, rustic *trattoria* offers a range of meat- and fish-based dishes, along with excellent pizzas and a good choice of wines.

Healing Gardens
Just to the side of San Marco and attached to the University's Natural History Museum, the delightful Giardino dei Semplici (Botanical Garden; Mon–Tue, Thur–Fri 9am–1pm, Sat 9am–5pm; charge) was begun by Duke Cosimo in 1545. Initially it was used to grow medicinal herbs, but today tropical plants and Tuscan flora have been added to the collection.

unofficial rulers of Florence until Piero fled the city in 1494. The courtyard walls are studded with antique inscriptions, and the renovated **Cappella dei Magi** is home to the stunningly colourful fresco of Benozzo Gozzoli's *Journey of the Magi* (1459), in which members of the Medici family are depicted among the royal retinue.

PIAZZA SAN MARCO

Emerging from the Palazzo Medici-Riccardi, turn left and continue up Via Cavour to **Piazza San Marco** ❽. In term time you will weave your way through chatting groups of art students who study at the Accademia, which was founded in 1563 by Vasari, with

Michelangelo as one of its original members. Now you have a choice: if you are feeling weary, you may want to finish here and head off for some refreshment. On Piazza San Marco itself is **Accademia**, see ⑪⑤, which is a good retreat, or you could try the scrumptious ice creams at **Gelateria Carabé**, see ⑪⑥. If, however, it is a Saturday or Sunday, and you have the energy, then you can carry on to explore the treasures of the Museo di San Marco.

Church and Museum of San Marco

At the head of the square is the church of **San Marco** ❾ (Mon–Sat 8.30am–noon and 4–6pm, Sun 4–6pm), which was remodelled by Michelozzo from 1437 onwards. The interior is decorative, but of more interest are the peaceful cloisters and monastic buildings attached to it that make up the fascinating **Museo di San Marco** ❿ (tel: 055-238 8608; www.polomuseale. firenze.it; Mon–Fri 8.15am–1.20pm, Sat–Sun 8.15am–4.20pm, closed 1st, 3rd and 5th Sun and 2nd and 4th Monday in the month; charge).

Many famous names are connected with San Marco. Cosimo de' Medici paid for the building of this monastery, which was originally (from 1436) occupied by Dominican friars from the nearby hill town of Fiesole. Fra Angelico spent most of his life within its walls, and the museum contains many of his paintings; his *Crucifixion* (1442) is in the Chapter House.

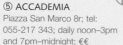

Food and Drink

⑤ ACCADEMIA
Piazza San Marco 8r; tel: 055-217 343; daily noon–3pm and 7pm–midnight; €€
Opposite the front of the church of San Marco, this restaurant is both a haven from cultural overload and a convivial setting where pizzas, pasta and other food are washed down with the good house wine.

⑥ GELATERIA CARABÉ
Via Ricasoli 60r; tel: 055-289 476; May–Sept: daily 10am–midnight, Oct–Apr: Tue–Sun 10am–8pm; €
This place is not to be missed if you are a fan of ice cream. Sicilian *gelati* are made from ingredients shipped in from the island itself.

The Dormitory

The **Dormitorio** is the high point of the museum, consisting of 44 monastic cells under a great open roof. Fra Angelico's *Annunciation* is located at the top of the stairs. Beyond, each cell contains a small fresco that is stripped to its essential religious significance; they were intended as aids to contemplation. The frescoes in cells 1 to 10, on the left, are probably the work of Fra Angelico; the rest are by his assistants. In cell 7, the *Mocking of Christ* is typical of his style, where disembodied hands beat Christ about the head. Savonarola *(see p.38)* believed in the futility of earthly deeds and passions and saw only the afterlife as important, so, fittingly, cells 12 to 14 contain his hair shirt, as well as a copy of a contemporary painting of his execution.

The other wing of the Dormitory leads past the **Biblioteca** (Library), a graceful hall built to house the illuminated manuscripts donated by Cosimo de'Medici to create Europe's first public library, and designed by Michelozzo in 1441. The cells that Cosimo reserved for his own retreats (nos 38 and 39) are at the end of the corridor. The wall of cell 39 is decorated with the *Three Kings and their retinue visiting the Nativity*, in a scene painted by Benozzo Gozzoli.

Above from far left: San Marco backstreet; nuns and priest taking a stroll.

Below: restoration at San Marco.

THE ACCADEMIA TO THE MUSEO ARCHEOLOGICO

This tour takes you from the collection of Michelangelo's sculpture in the Accademia, via the beautiful square of Santissima Annunziata with its Brunelleschi buildings, to the superb Archaeological Museum.

DISTANCE 300m (¼ mile)
TIME A full day
START Galleria dell'Accademia
END Museo Archeologico
POINTS TO NOTE

This walk starts where tour 5 ends, on Piazza San Marco. On a weekday, when the Museo di San Marco closes early *(see p.56)*, it would be possible to join the two routes together, starting here with the museum before moving on to the Accademia. However, to try and combine the two routes in total would be far too long for a single day's sightseeing.

Food and Drink
① ROBIGLIO
Via dei Servi 112; tel: 055-212 784; Mon–Sat 8am–8pm; €
This is one of the chain of Robiglio cafés serving delicious pastries and chocolates as well as tasty lunches. Do try the squidgy choux buns.

This short route packs a lot into a small geographical area. The highlight for many will be a sight of the restored original of Michelangelo's *David* in the Galleria dell'Accademia, as opposed to the copy in front of the Palazzo Vecchio.

THE ACCADEMIA

Start the tour at Piazza San Marco, on the far side of which, at Via Ricasoli 58, is the **Galleria dell' Accademia ❶** (tel: 055-238 8609; www.polomuseale. firenze.it; Tue–Sun 8.15am–6.50pm; charge). This gallery attracts a huge number of visitors, and long queues can build up, especially at Easter and in the summer. If you find a queue has already formed, don't despair – it moves quite quickly. There is no café in the museum itself, but if you are in need of refreshment before going in, then head for **Robiglio**, see ⑪①, on Via dei Servi close to Piazza Santissima.

The Collection
The Accademia's collection contains sculpture and early Renaissance religious art, and has been expanded to

include a display of musical instruments. On entry, the Sala del Colosso showcases the plaster cast of Giambologna's *Rape of the Sabine Women* (on display in the Loggia dei Lanzi, *see p.36*) and a collection of colourful religious art from the early Cinquecento (16th century).

The door located to the left of the entrance takes you into the gallery proper, starting with the **Galleria dei Prigionieri**, where Michelangelo's fine unfinished *Four Slaves* (*c.*1530), originally intended for the tomb of Pope Julius II, are displayed. The view from here of *David (see box on p.60)*, in the domed **Tribuna di Michelangelo**, is absolutely stunning.

Off to the left of the Tribuna di Michelangelo are three small rooms –

the **Sala del Duecento e Prima Trecento**, the **Sala di Giotto e della sua scuola** and the **Sala di Giovanni da Milano e degli Orcagna**. These all hold early Florentine works, some by Gaddi and Daddi. The *Tree of Life* (*c.*1310) by Buonaguida is a highlight. At the end of the hall the Salone dell'Ottocento is packed with plaster busts and statues once used by Accademia students.

Stairs lead to the first floor and four further rooms. The first two exhibit attractive work from the late 14th century. The following room is dedicated to Florentine painter Lorenzo Monaco, whose work expresses the bridge between Gothic and Renaissance art, which is the key to understanding the Florentine style.

Above from far left: exterior of the Accademia; sculpted torso, Accademia; a great way to get around the city; elaborate ceiling in the Spedale degli Innocenti.

The University

On the northeastern side of Piazza San Marco are the buildings now occupied by the administrative offices of the Università, originally built as stables for the horses and wild animals kept by Duke Cosimo I.

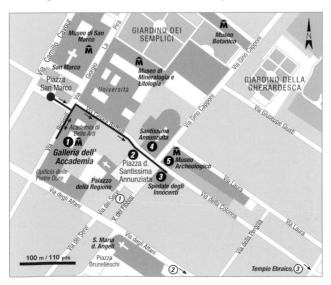

Back downstairs, adjoining the lobby, the **Sala del Colosseo** displays the full-size plaster model of Giambologna's *Rape of the Sabine Women*, the marble version of which stands in the Loggia of the Palazzo Vecchio. From here a short hallway brings you to the **Dipartimento degli Srumentali Musicali**, with musical instruments from the 17th to 19th centuries. Highlights are a Stradivari violin, a cello by Amati and the world's oldest surviving upright piano.

HOSPITAL OF THE INNOCENTS

Turn right out of the Accademia and then right again into Via Cesare Battisti. This leads to the pedestrianised **Piazza della Santissima Annunziata** ❷, one of the most beautiful squares in Florence. In the centre of the square is an equestrian statue of *Duke Ferdinand I*, by Giambologna; this is partnered by two bronze fountains (by Pietro Tacca, 1608) featuring rather strange-looking marine monsters.

On the right-hand side of the square is the gracious colonnade of the **Spedale degli Innocenti** ❸, started by Brunelleschi in 1419 and the first classical loggia of its type. Here the columns of *pietra serena* (grey sandstone) alternate with Luca della Robbia's blue-and-white terracotta roundels that depict a baby in swad-

David

Michelangelo's *David* was sculpted between 1501 and 1504, and, through its depiction of the young boy who slew Goliath, it symbolises the birth of republican Florence. Originally situated in front of the Palazzo Vecchio (a copy, *pictured*, stands *in situ*), the statue, which stands at over 4m (13ft), was moved to the Accademia in 1873 for reasons of preservation; a decision that was heavily criticised at the time. The marble from which *David* was carved was famously rejected as faulty by other artists, but the then 29-year-old Michelangelo sought to embrace its faults and patches of discoloration. *David* is celebrated for being of perfect proportions when viewed from below and is hailed as a testament to Michelangelo's eye for detail: just see the muscle contour of the legs and the veins in the arms (even more apparent since the controversial clean up in 2004), which can be admired from every angle thanks to the way the statue is displayed. The eyes are of particular interest for their heart-shaped pupils.

dling clothes – the symbol of the Innocenti orphanage located just behind. The orphanage, opened in 1444 and the first in the world, is still used for its original purpose.

The building also houses the **Galleria dello Spedale degli Innocenti** (tel: 055-203 7308; daily 10am–7pm; charge), a gallery of pictures donated by patrons, including Ghirlandaio's *Adoration of the Magi* (1488). Brunelleschi's portico was copied on the opposite side of the square, where it now fronts a fine hotel, the Loggiato dei Serviti.

SANTISSIMA ANNUNZIATA

On the north side of the square is the grand entrance to the church of **Santissima Annunziata** ❹ (tel: 055-266 181; daily 8am–noon and 4.30–6.30pm; free). This contains some fine frescoes, such as Andrea del Sarto's *Birth of the Virgin* (1514) and, in the adjacent Chiostro dei Morti (Cloister of the Dead), his *Holy Family*.

ARCHEOLOGICAL MUSEUM

Turn left out of the church and cross the road for the **Museo Archeologico** ❺ (Piazza Santissima Annunziata 9b, tel: 055-23575; Mon 2–7pm, Wed and Thur 8.30am–7pm, Tue, Fri–Sun 8.30am–2pm; charge).

The first floor is partly given over to the exceptional Etruscan collections and temporary exhibitions. The tomb sculp-

ture gives a touching insight into the everyday lives of these peaceful people. The real stars of the museum, however, are the Etruscan bronzes. The 5th-century BC *Chimera*, part-lion, part-goat and part-snake, was discovered in Arezzo in 1554 and greatly admired by Renaissance bronze-casters, including Benvenuto Cellini, who was entrusted with the restoration of a broken foreleg. The *Arringatore* (2nd century BC) was discovered in Trasimeno in 1556.

Also on the first floor are Egyptian treasures while the revamped second floor is dedicated to ancient Greek, Etruscan and Roman art.

Options for eating are fairly limited in the immediate vicinity. You can either head south down Via dei Fibbai and then right into Via degli Alfani for **Lo Skipper**, see ⑪② or carry on down Via della Colonna, then turn right into Via Luigi Carlo Farini to **Ruth's**, see ⑪③.

Above from far left:
Spedale degli Innocenti; the grand, neoclassical Museo Archeologico.

The Synagogue
Florence's huge Tempio Ebraico (Sun–Thur 10am–1pm and 2–4pm, Fri 10am–1pm; charge), is easily recognised by its green, copper-covered dome. It was built in the Hispano-Moresque style between 1874 and 1882 on the site of the ghetto founded by Cosimo I in 1551.

Food and Drink

② LO SKIPPER
Via degli Alfani; tel: 055-284 019; Mon–Fri noon–2.30pm and 6.30–10.30pm, Sat and Sun 6.30–10.30pm; €€
With a concentration on fish dishes, this restaurant, run by a nautical club, offers good Italian food as well as dishes inspired by other culinary traditions, such as Mexican and Greek. Off the main tourist route.

③ RUTH'S
Via Luigi Carlo Farini 2a; tel: 055-248 0888; Sun–Thur 12.30–2.30pm, 7.30–10pm, Fri 12.30–2.30pm, Sat 7.30–10pm; €
Next to the grand synagogue, this little place is one of the few to cater for vegetarians. It offers a range of kosher and Middle Eastern-style dishes from falafel to couscous and hummus.

AROUND PIAZZA DELLA REPUBBLICA

The roads to the west of Florence's grand 19th-century Piazza della Repubblica are home to many of the city's designer shops, including famous Florentine names such as Gucci, Pucci and Ferragamo.

DISTANCE 1km (½ mile)
TIME A half day
START Piazza della Repubblica
END Mercato Nuovo
POINTS TO NOTE
This tour is best done in the morning, if you want to see inside the Palazzo Davanzati. Be sure to book ahead if you intend to visit the Ferragamo Shoe Museum.

Food and Drink 🍴

① GIUBBE ROSSE
Piazza della Repubblica 13/14r; tel: 055-212 280; Thur–Tue 7.30am–1am; €€€
Florence's famous literary café is more touristy now. It offers *panini* and a lunch buffet or an upmarket dinner menu.

② GILLI
Piazza della Repubblica 36–39; tel: 055-213 896; Wed–Mon 7.30am–10pm; €€–€€€
This elegant place claims to be Florence's oldest café. It is also a luxurious *chocolaterie*.

③ PASZKOWSKI
Piazza della Repubblica 31–35r; tel: 055-210 236; Tue–Sun 9am–1.30am; €€–€€€
This grand café is great for coffee and cake, lunch, or after-dinner drinks accompanied by live music.

This walk around the elegant streets west of the city centre takes in the boutiques of Florence's most famous designers. Begin the tour, however, at the large open square of **Piazza della Repubblica ❶**.

PIAZZA DELLA REPUBBLICA

Built on the site of the Roman forum, this square formed the centrepiece of the 19th-century rebuilding project that sought to transform Florence into a capital fit for the new United Kingdom of Italy. As it turned out, the city was only the capital between 1865 and 1871, and the redevelopment of the old ghetto was halted by the outcry from foreign afficionados of the narrow streets and medieval architecture. All that remains of the grand plan is the piazza, and the grand triumphal arch bearing an inscription to the effect that 'the ancient heart of the city was restored to new life from its former squalor in 1895'.

The square and its immediate surroundings form a pleasant contrast to the sometimes rather stark streets of the

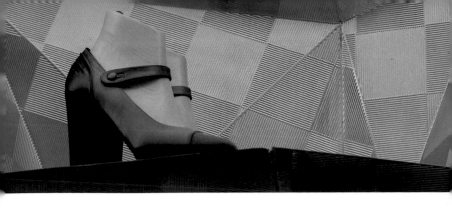

old city. More importantly, it is also home to some swish cafés, in which you can have a coffee before starting your walk. The three most famous are the **Giubbe Rosse**, see ⓘ①, **Gilli**, see ⓘ②, and **Paszkowski**, see ⓘ③.

STROZZI PALACE

Once fortified, take the western exit from the square along Via degli Strozzi. At the second turning on the left is Piazza Strozzi, location of the **Palazzo Strozzi** ❷ (tel: 055-264 5155; www. palazzostrozzi.org; open during exhibitions daily 10am–8pm, Thur to 11pm; charge). This was the last, and largest, of the Renaissance palaces built in the city. Constructed by the banker Filippo Strozzi between 1489 and 1536, the

building of what was an even bigger palace than the Medici's Palazzo Medici-Riccardi *(see p.55)* bankrupted the family. The façade has a huge classical cornice, and the massive stone walls have Renaissance torch holders and lamp brackets. The interior courtyard was greatly remodelled during the 19th century and is relatively charmless, but it has a café and a small museum that shows how the palace once looked. The palace is now used to hold major temporary exhibitions and also contains the Gabinetto Vieusseux public library.

VIA DE' TORNABUONI

At the end of Via degli Strozzi turn left into **Via de' Tornabuoni** ❸. Florence's most upmarket shopping streets.

Above from far left: Piazza della Repubblica; expect to pass some fine shoe shops on this tour.

Watching the Workers
Filippo Strozzi could keep an eye on the progress of the construction of his huge mansion from the original family palace – itself no mean dwelling – just across the street.

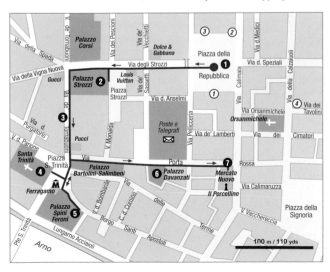

Above from left: Sala dei Papagalli in Palazzo Davanzati; inspecting the leather goods at the Mercato Nuovo.

Palaces here house the showrooms of the likes of Pucci, Ferragamo, Armani, Gucci and Prada, while the latter is home to such names as Valentino, Versace and La Perla. Florence has long been known for its fabrics, leather and superb craftsmanship, which helped it to become fabulously wealthy during the Renaissance.

Santa Trinità

At the end of Via de' Tornabuoni is busy Piazza Santa Trinità and, on the right, the church of **Santa Trinità** ➍ (tel: 055-216 912; daily 7am–noon and 4–7pm; free). Here, the relative austerity of the 13th-century Gothic interior contrasts with the Baroque façade and Ghirlandaio's stunningly colourful frescoes and altarpiece of the Sassetti Chapel, to the right of the choir. The frescoes (1483) illustrate the *Life of St Francis,* and the altarpiece (1485) shows the *Nativity.* Other frescoes depict scenes from Classical lit-erature and mythology, set against a Florentine backdrop.

Ferragamo Museum

Opposite the church is the **Palazzo Spini-Feroni** ➎, one of the city's few remaining 13th-century palaces. Its ground floor is now home to the flagship store of Salvatore Ferragamo. The famous shoe designer used to live in the palace and, above the shop, the small but excellent **Museo Ferragamo** (tel: 055-336 0456; www.salvatoreferragamo.it; Wed–Mon 10am–6pm; charge) has an exhibition on his life and work, as well as some spectacular shoes.

DAVANZATI PALACE

Now take Via Porta Rossa, behind the Palazzo Spini-Feroni, to the **Palazzo Davanzati** ➏ (tel: 055-238 8610; daily 8.15am–1.50pm, closed 2nd and 4th Sun and 3rd and 5th Mon in the month; the two upper floors are visited in guided

---

Food and Drink 🍴

④ CANTINETTA DEI VERRAZZANO

Via dei Tavolini 18r; tel: 055-268 590; Sept–Jun: Mon–Sat 8am–9pm, Jul–Aug: 8am–4pm; €

This is part bakery, part *enoteca.* The bakery has special flavoured breads, pastries and tiny pizzas. Sit in the *enoteca* for a glass of Chianti and some *pecorino* cheese with balsamic vinegar, or an assortment of *foccaccia* with *prosciutto.*

Right: entrance to the Palazzo Davanzati.

groups only at 10am, 11am and noon, by appointment; charge). The façade dates from the mid-14th century and is typical of Tuscan pre-Renaissance architecture, including features such as the so-called depressed arch over the doors and windows. The coat of arms is that of the Davanzati family, who owned the palace from 1518 until 1538. The open loggia that crowns the palace was added in the 16th century. Now restored the house gives a fascinating insight into life in medieval Florence.

Highlights

Inside is a beautiful courtyard and an elegant stone staircase supported by flying arches. Note the well to the right of the entrance with a pulley system enabling buckets of water to be lifted to each of the five floors – a private water supply was a considerable luxury.

The principal living rooms occupy the first floor, the *piano nobile*, where you will find the gorgeously frescoed dining room, the **Sala dei Papagalli** (Room of the Parrots) after the birds pictured in the borders.

The bedchambers on the floors above also have murals, notably the one decorated with scenes from the 13th-century French romance, the *Châtelaine de Vergy*. Although the furnishings in each room – beds, chests and stools – may look sparse, they represent a considerable degree of luxury for the time, as do the private bathrooms off each room, complete with

toilets and terracotta waste pipes. In the kitchen situated on the top floor you will find an array of contemporary utensils, including equipment for kneading and shaping pasta.

MERCATO NUOVO

At the end of Via Porta Rossa, on the right, is the **Mercato Nuovo** **❼** (New Market). A market has existed here since the 11th century, and the 'new' current arcade was built between 1547 and 1551 for the sale of silk and gold. Later it gained the name 'straw market' (Mercato della Paglia) from the woven-straw *(raffia)* goods sold there by peasants. Leather goods and T-shirts now form the bulk of the its offerings.

For something to eat, if you do not fancy the tripe stand *(see margin, right)*, you can always return to the cafés on Piazza della Repubblica or head a little further east to Via dei Tavolini to the **Cantinetta dei Verrazzano**, see ⑪④, for some tasty nibbles.

Tasty Tripe
At the southwest corner of the Mercato Nuovo is a very popular tripe stand. Here you can pick delicacies such as *trippa alla fiorentina* (tripe in tomato sauce) and *lampredotto,* a sandwich filled with meat from a cow's fourth stomach.

Il Porcellino

Located south of the Mercato Nuovo, Il Porcellino attracts countless visitors who come to rub the snout of this bronze boar that was copied from the Roman statue in the Uffizi, itself a copy of an Hellenic original. The statue you see today is actually yet another copy; its predecessor was sent for restoration in 1998. It is said that anyone who rubs the snout is certain to return to the city. Coins dropped in the trough below are distributed to city charities.

OLTRARNO

On the south side of the Arno is the laid-back district of Oltrarno, where a wealth of sights, including the stunning frescoes in the Brancacci Chapel, as well as some lovely restaurants and bars, can be found.

DISTANCE 1.5km (1 mile)
TIME A half day
START Santa Felicità
END Porta San Frediano
POINTS TO NOTE

If you wanted to make a full day of this tour, then it could be combined with a visit to the Palazzo Pitti and Boboli Garden (walk 9, *see pp.70–3*) by adding these sights from the Piazza de'Pitti. Bear in mind, though, that this would make for a lot of sightseeing.

Oltrarno literally means 'beyond the Arno', and this tour takes in some of the most important sights in the neighbourhoods on the southern bank of Florence's river. First brought inside the city walls in the 14th century, this area still feels a little separate from the rest of Florence.

SANTA FELICITÀ

Begin on the southern side of the Ponte Vecchio. Before you start it might be worth popping along to Piazza dei Rossi (at the far end of

Food and Drink

① LE VOLPI E L'UVA
Piazza dei Rossi 1; tel: 055-239 8132; Mon–Sat 11am–9pm; €
This superb little wine bar has a fabulous selection of Italian wines, including quite a number of little-known vintages from small producers. They also serve very tasty plates of cheese and *salumi*, as well as *schiacciatine* (thin flat bread) and hot *focaccia* topped with mushrooms and *prosciutto*.

② OSTERIA SANTO SPIRITO
Piazza Santo Spirito 16r; tel: 055-238 2383; daily 12.45–2.30pm and 8pm–midnight; €€€
A somewhat trendy hang-out with colourful decor and noisy music. The food is inventive, and fish figures largely. Be sure to order some of the excellent pasta on offer; the *orecchiette* is recommended.

③ BORGO ANTICO
Piazza Santo Spirito 6r; tel: 055-210 437; daily 12.30–3pm and 8–11.30pm; €€
A cosy restaurant with a standard menu and an extensive range of daily specials. Try the ravioli for a rich, filling pasta dish, or one of the *secondi* from the specials menu.

Piazza Santa Felicità), where you can get a drink and something to eat at the lovely *enoteca* **Le Volpi e l'Uva**, see ⑪①.

From the bridge, walk down Via de'Guicciardini to the church of **Santa Felicità** ❶ (tel: 055-213 018; Mon–Sat 9.30am–noon and 3.30–5.30pm; Sun 9am–1pm; free), on the left. Take a look inside this church, which has two remarkable works by the Mannerist artist, Pontormo, an *Annunciation* and a *Deposition* (both 1525–8). Their colours are almost acidic in their vividness and a contrast to the more subdued hues used by Renaissance painters.

Turn left out of the church and walk down to the Piazza de'Pitti. Dominating the square is the huge Palazzo Pitti. This, and the Boboli Garden just behind, are explored in walk 9 *(see p.70)*.

CASA GUIDI

On the far (southern) corner of Piazza de'Pitti look out for the first-floor **Casa Guidi** ❷ (Guidi House; tel: 055-354 457/055-284 393; Jan–Feb and Apr–Nov: Mon, Wed and Fri 3–6pm; donations welcome), at Piazza San Felice 8. It is located inside the 15th-century Palazzo Guidi, where the poets Robert and Elizabeth Browning lived from 1847 (shortly after their secret marriage) until Elizabeth's death in 1861. It was Elizabeth who called the apartment 'Casa Guidi' to change 'a mere palace into a home'. It is also

available to rent via the Landmark Trust (www.landmarktrust.org.uk).

PIAZZA SANTO SPIRITO

From here, turn into Via Mazzetta, which leads into Piazza Santo Spirito where there is a small market each morning from Monday to Saturday. The square is a good place to get something to eat, and two places worth trying are the **Osteria Santo Spirito**, see ⑪②, and **Borgo Antico**, see ⑪③.

There are many good antiques shops nearby, especially around Via Maggio. This part of the city is very different from the historic centre – bustling, lively and authentically Florentine.

Santo Spirito

At the head of the square is the church of **Santo Spirito** ❸ (tel: 055-210 030;

Above from far left: local artisan shopkeeper; view towards Oltrarno.

Early Church
Santa Felicità stands on the site of a late-Roman church, thought to have been built in the 3rd or 4th century AD by Eastern merchants at a time when Christians were still liable to persecution. The church was rebuilt during the 16th century, and again in 1736.

Masaccio

Born Tomasso Cassai (1401–78), Masaccio is credited with the invention of scientific perspective, whereby lines of sight in a painting disappear towards a single point of reference. This enabled him to give his works a greater realism than those of earlier painters. Another of his innovations was the lighting of a picture from a single source, so creating a more realistic chiaroscuro (interplay of light and shade).

Brunelleschi's Limpets

A total of 40 chapels with side-altars and paintings radiate from the aisles and transepts of Santo Spirito. If Brunelleschi's design had been executed in full, these would have formed a ring of conical-roofed apses around the exterior of the church, clinging like a cluster of limpets to the main structure.

Mon–Tue and Thur–Sat 10am–12.30pm and 4pm–5.30pm, Wed 10am–noon, Sun 11.30am–noon; free). Begun in 1436, it was regarded as Brunelleschi's masterpiece and is a superb example of Renaissance Classicism. Among the works of art on display in the church, note Filippino Lippi's *Madonna and Saints* (*c.*1490), in the right-hand transept.

Adjacent is the **Cenacolo di Santo Spirito** (tel: 055-287 043; Sat, Apr–Oct: 9am–5pm, Nov–Mar: 10.30am–1.30pm; charge), the refectory, which contains Orcagna's 14th-century fresco *The Last Supper*. Although the work

was damaged in the 18th century, the outer part can still be seen. Above it is a more complete *Crucifixion*.

BRANCACCI CHAPEL

Walk back to the piazza, turn right into Via Sant'Agostino and continue down Via Santa Monaca to reach Piazza del Carmine. The church of **Santa Maria del Carmine** ❹ was destroyed by fire in 1771, and subsequently rebuilt. However the **Cappella Brancacci** ❺ tel: 055-276 8224; Mon, Wed–Sat 10am–5pm, Sun 1–5pm; charge), just to the right, was spared. A maximum

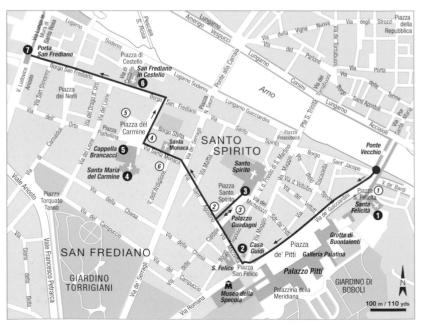

of 30 visitors are allowed in at one time for only 15 minutes and reservations are advised in high season. The ticket includes a 40-minute film in English.

Once inside this tiny chapel you are brought face to face with the restored frescoes on the *Life of St Peter*, begun by Masolino, continued by Masaccio *(see box, p.67)* from 1425 until his death in 1428, and completed by Filippino Lippi in 1480. Masaccio's contribution has been hailed as a superb example of the emerging Renaissance style, remarkable for his use of perspective and chiaroscuro to highlight the central figures. A serene St Peter moves among the poor and crippled, distributing alms and working miracles, against the backdrop of 15th-century Florence.

Masaccio's work is mainly in the upper tier of the fresco and includes his *Expulsion from Paradise*, in which the figures of Adam and Eve, no longer beautiful as in Masolino's *Temptation* scene opposite, are racked with misery. The scenes in the lower tier, mostly by Filippino Lippi, are equally distinguished.

SAN FREDIANO

Across the expansive Piazza del Carmine, spoilt by its use as a car park, lies Borgo San Frediano. This is the principal street of a characterful, traditionally working-class district. A little way down is the church of **San Frediano ❻** (tel: 055-215 816; daily 9am–noon and 4.30–5.30pm, Sun to 6pm; free). It has an unfinished rough stone façade but possesses one of the finest Baroque interiors in Florence. The frescoed dome over the main altar is by Antonio Domenico Gabbiani. Also notable are the 14th-century *Madonna of the Smile* and, in the refectory, Bernardino Poccetti's *Last Supper* (*c.*1600).

At the western end of the Borgo is **Porta San Frediano ❼**, built in 1324 and one of the best-preserved stretches of the 14th-century city walls.

This part of the city has quite a number of decent places to eat, and at the end of your tour you could head for **Dolce Vita**, see ⑪④, **Napoleone**, see ⑪⑤, or the **Cavolo Nero**, see ⑪⑥.

Food and Drink

④ DOLCE VITA

Piazza del Carmine; tel: 055-284 595; Mon–Sat 10am–2am, Sun 5pm–2am, *aperitivo* daily 7.30–9.30pm; €€
This trendy, often busy bar, with cool interiors and live music (Wed–Thur), is beloved by Florentine students, who come here for the *aperitivo* and its great cocktails.

⑤ NAPOLEONE

Piazza del Carmine 24; tel: 055-281 015; daily 7pm–1am; €€
This colourful *trattoria*, with a quirky but modern interior, is set in a quiet location near the church. It serves decent traditional Tuscan dishes such as steaks, salads and plates of *salumi*.

⑥ CAVOLO NERO

Via dell'Ardiglione 22; tel: 055-294 744; Mon–Sat 7pm–midnight; €€€
The elegant-looking 'Black Cabbage' (a vital ingredient in *ribollita*) specialises in Mediterranean food such as couscous salad, gazpacho, grilled octopus and some great handmade pasta. The place is not on the main tourist trail, though it is well known from its rising popularity with guidebooks.

9

THE PITTI PALACE AND BOBOLI GARDEN

Taken over by the Medici when its owner went bust, the huge Pitti Palace is now home to some exceptional works of art, but perhaps its jewel in the crown is the lovely Boboli Garden.

Above: shady avenue and blooms in the Boboli Garden.

DISTANCE 1km (½ mile)
TIME A full day
START Pitti Palace
END Boboli Garden
POINTS TO NOTE

It might be possible to fit this tour in with the general Oltrarno walk (no. 8) but it would mean rushing around the Palatine Gallery and gardens, as well as missing out on the other museums in the palace.

It is easy to spend a full day, or more, over this tour. As well as a stunning collection of art, there are museums of fashion, porcelain and silver, as well as the beautiful Boboli Garden – one of the highlights of a trip to Florence.

PITTI PALACE

The tour begins on Piazza de'Pitti, in front of the imposing, and somewhat austere, façade of the **Palazzo Pitti ❶**.

The palace was begun in the late 1450s for the banker Luca Pitti, but the cost of the building brought him to the verge of bankruptcy, and, after his death, his heirs sold it to Eleonora di Toledo, the Spanish-born wife of Duke Cosimo I, in 1549. The Medici family moved here in 1550, and from then on it served as the home of Tuscany's rulers, gradually being expanded to its present immense bulk.

PALATINE GALLERY

Start in the left wing of the first floor of the palace, home to the **Galleria Palatina** (tel: 055-294 883; www.polo museale.firenze.it; Tue–Sun 8.15am–6.50pm; charge). This gallery contains some outstanding works of art hung in beautiful rooms. The ticket office is in the right wing, and the entrance to the gallery is off the internal courtyard.

The gallery begins with a series of antechambers containing some notable paintings. Filippo Lippi's beautiful tondo of the *Madonna and Child* and Rubens' *Three Graces* hang in the Sala di Prometeo (room 14) and the Sala dei Putti respectively. The Sala di Bagno (Bathroom), decorated with stucco nymphs and four marble

Nereides, was designed for the French Emperor Napoleon, after he had conquered northern Italy.

Mythological Decoration

The most splendid apartments overlook the main piazza. The regal setting of these six rooms is matched by masterpieces on the walls by Raphael, Rubens and Titian. The Sala dell' Illiade (room 27) is one of the most sumptuous in the palace, with a frescoed neoclassical ceiling inspired by Homeric myths. The splendid Sala di Saturno (room 28) is wall-to-wall with masterpieces, including some of Raphael's finest works; it also has a fine 17th-century ceiling, depicting an Olympian scene in gilt and stuccowork.

The adjoining Sala di Giove (room 29) has the grandeur befitting a Medici throne room and is decorated with Pietro da Cortona's frescoes glorifying the young Prince Ferdinando. The ceiling is supported by a seething mass of nymphs, gods and entwined cherubs, while the far door is framed by masterpieces painted by Raphael *(Woman with a Veil)*, and Giorgione. Next, the Sala di Marte (Room 30) contains an array of Flemish and Italian masterpieces, set against vibrant red damask walls, including Rubens' great martial work, *The Consequences of War* (1637).

The Sala di Apollo (room 31), which is frescoed and dotted with statuary, is equally ornate. Framing the entrance doorway are masterpieces by Titian, such as his luminous *Mary Magdalene*, a nude wreathed in the artist's trademark Titian hair.

Above from far left:
Boboli Garden views; Pitti Palace.

Palace Owners
After Medici rule ended in 1737, the palace became the home of the Lorraines – tho ostentatious decor dates from this period – and then the Savoys. There was a brief tenure by the Bourbons and Napoleon before the last ruling monarch, Vittorio Emmanuele III, transferred the building to the public.

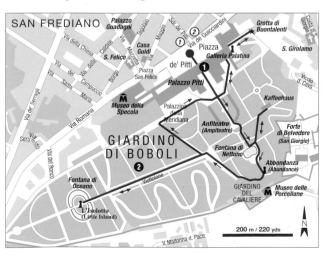

Above: Boboli Garden statues.

Supreme Views
The bastions of the Boboli Garden were designed by Michelangelo. The view, taking in the city and the Tuscan countryside beyond, is one of the most beautiful in Florence.

The Sala di Venere (room 32) is named after Canova's *Venus Italica* (*c.*1812), commissioned by Napoleon as a replacement for the Hellenistic *Venus de' Medici* that he had spirited away to Paris. Canova's masterpiece of neoclassical statuary is the companion piece to the *Venus*, which is now in the Uffizi (see p.42).

Royal Apartments

On the first floor in the right wing, beyond the Galleria Palatina, are the **Appartamente Reali** (Royal Apartments). Only some of these rooms are open at any one time. These are rather ostentatious rooms, with plush and heavy carpets and draped fabrics. Several are named after the colour in which they are decorated, and contain paintings and portraits; there are also the Queen's Apartments, the King's Apartments and a ceremonial room, all filled with exquisite furniture.

NICHE MUSEUMS

In addition to the Galleria Palatina there are four other museums in the Palazzo Pitti (tel: 055-294 883; www.polomuseale.firenze.it). A cumulative ticket is available for all four.

Decorative Arts Museum
On the ground floor, the **Museo degli Argenti** (Silver Museum; daily, Nov–Feb: 8.15am–4.30pm, Mar and Oct: 8.15am–5.30pm, Apr–May and Sept–Oct: 8.15am–6.30pm, Jun–Aug: 8.15am– 6.50pm; closed first and last Mon of the month, last entrance one hour before closure; charge) is in the left-hand corner of the courtyard, while the **Museo delle Porcellane** (Porcelain Museum; same times and ticket as the Museo degli Argenti) is situated in the Boboli Garden. The former contains silver and other baubles collected by the Medicis; the latter some fine porcelain.

Modern Art and Costume Galleries
The second floor houses the **Galleria d'Arte Moderna** (same times and ticket as the Galleria Palatina), which contains mainly neoclassical and Romantic and Impressionist Italian works of art.

Also on the second floor is the **Galleria del Costume** (same times and ticket as the Museo degli Argenti), whose 6,000-piece holding of clothing, theatrical costumes and accessories are supplemented by special exhibitions.

Food and Drink 🍴

① CAFFE PITTI
Piazza de'Pitti 9; tel: 055-239 9863; daily noon–11pm; €€
This venue located directly opposite the Palazzo Pitti is a popular hang-out for locals and tourists alike. Truffles are a speciality of the house, served with pasta or tenderloin steak. Truffle tastings take place here in November and December.

② PITTI GOLA E CANTINA
Piazza de'Pitti 16; tel: 055-212 704; daily 1pm–midnight; €
Lined with shelving bearing innumerable bottles of wine, many available by the glass, this is a great little *enoteca*. To try the wine tasting dinner make sure to book ahead.

BOBOLI GARDEN

Just behind the palace is the formal **Giardino di Boboli** ❷ (same times and ticket as Museo degli Argenti). The garden is entered from the inner courtyard via a flight of steps that leads to a terrace to the rear of the palace in front of Susini's fountain, constructed in 1641. The fountain sits at the focal point of a grassy amphitheatre, laid out from 1630 to 1635.

Statuary, Structures and Stonework
The huge granite basin nearby is from Rome's ancient Caracalla baths. A series of terraces leads up to Stoldo Lorenzi's *Neptune Fountain* (Fontana di Nettuno; 1565–9) and to the left is the Baroque **Kaffeehaus**, built in 1776 as a spot from which Duke Leopold's court could appreciate the views of Florence.

Heading back to the gardens, a path leads up to the statue of Abundance *(Abbondanza)*, then to the enclosed

Giardino del Cavaliere, constructed in 1529 and now restored with low box hedges, rose bushes and lovely views.

Walk past the gardeners' houses until you reach the top of the **Viottolone**, a shady, cypress avenue planted in 1637 and lined with lichen-covered antique statues. The *Fontana dell'Oceano* by Giambologna on the Isolotto (Little Island) and the crumbling statues encircling the lake, make this a magical spot.

Buontalenti Grotto
From the top of the Viottolone, a path takes you back to the east wing of the Pitti Palace via the smaller Palazzina della Meridiana and past the **Grotta di Buontalenti** (only with a guide, daily 11am, 1pm, 3pm, Apr–Sept: also 4pm and 5pm; free), a fantastic grotto with copies of Michelangelo's *Four Slaves* set in the four corners. Further inside, you will come across *Paris seducing Helen of Troy* in Vincenzo de' Rossi's erotic sculpture, and, almost out of sight at the rear of the cave, is Giambologna's *Venus* emerging from her bath. Before leaving don't miss the statue of the potbellied Pietro Barbino, Cosimo I's court dwarf, riding on a turtle, which is just by the east gate.

For a restorative meal with a truffle theme head for the **Caffè Pitti**, see 🍴①, opposite the palace on Piazza de' Pitti and open all day; or, close by, the **Pitti Gola e Cantina** see 🍴② is a great place for a glass of wine and tasty Tuscan fare.

Above from far left: statues dot the garden; relaxing in the sunshine.

Giardino Bardini
The Bardini Gardens, (Via dei Bardi 1 and Costa San Giorgio 2; same times and ticket as Museo degli Argenti; www.bardini peyron.it) now open to the public after restoration, rise up in terraces towards Piazzale Michelangelo. More peaceful than the Boboli Gardens they feature statues, fountains and fine views over Florence. The Villa Bardini (closed for restoration) features some extravagant creations by fashion designer Roberto Capucci. The gardens can also be accessed from Via dei Bardi, Piazza dei Mozzi, near the Museo Bardini (see p.74).

Left: Buontalenti Grotto, Boboli Garden.

SAN MINIATO AL MONTE

The fairly strenuous walk to the jewel-like church of San Miniato and the Piazzale Michelangelo is amply rewarded by sweeping views. Then meander down, passing villas and fields, to the Belvedere Fortress.

DISTANCE 5km (3 miles)
TIME A full day
START Ponte alle Grazie
END Via de'Bardi
POINTS TO NOTE
This route requires quite a bit of walking, some of it uphill, so it is best to devote a whole day to it and to take things quite slowly. Fortunately, there are some good places to stop and eat en route. Note the Museo Stefano Bardini is only open Fri–Mon.

Intellectual Neighbours
The villas that line the hills of the eastern part of Oltrarno were home to many of the artists, scientists and philosophers who have lived in the city. They included Galileo, who lived at the Villa il Gioiello (42 Via del Pian de' Giullari 42).

Food and Drink

① NEGRONI
Via dei Renai 17r; tel: 055-243 647; Mon–Fri 8am–3am, Sat and Sun 7pm–3am; €
This café by day, bar by night hosts a lively crowd. As well as being a very good place for an *aperitivo* – try the famous Negroni, for which the bar is named – it also serves tasty Mediterranean snacks and dishes.

② ANTICA MESTICA
Via di San Niccolò 60r; tel: 055-234 2836; Mon–Sat 12.30–3pm, 8–11pm; €
This *osteria* does simple and cheap, but extremely good, Italian food served up in a cheery, crowded atmosphere. Part of the eatery is set in a former chapel.

The lovely Romanesque church of San Miniato al Monte sits on a hill to the south of the city. The walk up to the church takes in Piazzale Michelangelo, justly famous for its views over Florence. On the way down, take in the Belvedere, a huge fortress now used for exhibitions.

Begin on the southern side of **Ponte alle Grazie** ❶. For a coffee before you start, turn left down Via dei Renai for the café-bar **Negroni**, see ⑪①.

BARDINI MUSEUM

Return towards the bridge and turn left to the small **Museo Stefano Bardini** ❷ (Piazza dei Mozzi 1; tel: 055-234 2427; Fri–Mon 11am–5pm, charge). Antiques dealer Stefano Bardini created his *palazzo* over the 13th-century church and monastery of San Gregorio in 1881, incorporating fragments of the ancient buildings. He used the rooms to showcase his vast art collection and bequeathed the palace and contents to the city in 1923. After 15 years of restoration the palace has been returned to its former glory. Among the highlights are Bernardo Daddi's monumental crucifix, a terracotta altarpiece by Andrea della Robbia, a Madonna

attributed to Donatello and Pollaiuolo's St Michael. There are also some lovely Persian carpets, Turkish ceramics, musical instruments and suits of armour. Bardini also created the nearby Giardino Bardini *(see margin p.73)*, also now open to the public.

SAN MINIATO GATEWAY

Turn left down Via di San Niccolò. This threads past imposing palaces and the church of San Niccolò, up to Via San Miniato, where you turn right and pass through the **Porta San Miniato** ❸. This is one of the few surviving gateways from the 14th-century city wall. If it is already lunch time, a good place for a bite to eat is the *osteria* **Antica Mestica**, see ⑪②, just before the arch.

On the other side of the arch turn left up Via dei Bastoni, which follows the wall. A short way up, look for a set of stone steps on the right that leads straight uphill, passing through leafy gardens and interrupted occa-

Above from far left: the fabulous view over Florence from San Miniato al Monte; architectural detail of the church's façade.

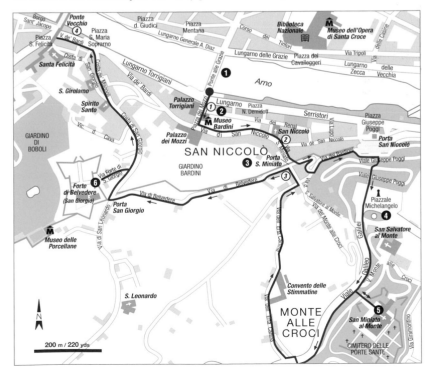

Miniato Mausoleum

Behind the church is a small graveyard that dates back to 1839. Family tombs are supplied with electricity to light the 'everlasting lamps', and there are many highly accomplished figures and portraits in stone and bronze of former Florentine citizens.

sionally by the switchback main road. Keep following these steps and paths as they weave upwards; on a clear day, the views are splendid. If you cannot face the climb, buses nos. 12 and 13 run from Ponte alle Grazie up to Piazzale Michelangelo.

PIAZZALE MICHELANGELO

At the top of the series of steps is the **Piazzale Michelangelo** ❹. The square was laid out in the 19th century and is dotted with reproductions of Michelangelo's sculptures, not to mention scores of tour buses and souvenir stalls. The views are stunning, it is from here that all those classic post-card pictures of the rooftops of Florence are taken.

Carry on up the busy Viale Galileo Galilei to the steps that lead up to the church of San Miniato.

SAN MINIATO AL MONTE

San Miniato al Monte ❺ (tel: 055-234 2731; daily, Apr–Oct: 8am–8pm, Nov–Mar: 8am–1pm and 3.30-7pm; free), and its convent buildings, is one of the most beautiful churches in Florence. Catch your breath while admiring the views from the terrace in front of the church and studying its delicate façade, which is covered in geometric patterns of green-and-white marble.

The church was built on the site of the tomb of the city's first Christian martyr, St Minias. He was executed in AD 250 during the anti-Christian purges of the Emperor Diocletian and his shrine was replaced by the present church in 1018. It incorporates Corinthian columns and other Roman material.

The Interior

The interior has survived more or less in its original state. Frescoes on the aisle

Right: the church and its adjacent convent building.

walls include a large 14th-century *St Christopher* by an unknown artist. The nave floor has a superb series of marble intarsia panels depicting lions, doves, signs of the zodiac and the date, 1207. To the left of the pulpit, behind an iron grille, is the tomb of the Cardinal of Portugal, who died on a visit to Florence in 1439. Its glazed terracotta ceiling is by Luca della Robbia. The mosaic in the apse (1297), shows Christ, the Virgin and St Minias. Try to time your trip to coincide with the Gregorian chant sung daily by the monks at 5.30pm.

THE DESCENT

Descend the steps back down to Viale Galileo Galilei and turn left. After about 150m/yds turn right into Via dell'Erta Canina. This winds down the hillside past villas, the **Convento delle Stimmatine** and fields that are filled with flowers in spring. At the bottom of the road turn right then left to the Porta San Miniato. Just before the gateway is the restaurant **Fuori Porta**, see ①③, which makes a pleasant lunch stop.

The Belvedere

To carry on, turn left immediately before Porta San Miniato and walk along Via di Belvedere until it meets Via di San Leonardo. Turn right, then left to bring you out in front of the **Forte di Belvedere ❻**. The sheer and massive walls of this fortress overlook the Boboli Garden. The interior, which

is still under restoration and usually closed, is almost empty and only used now for occasional exhibitions of contemporary and experimental art.

The fortress was built on the orders of Ferdinando I, beginning in 1590, to Buontalenti's design. Although the structure was said to be part of the city's defences, there was only one means of access – a secret door entered from the Boboli Garden – and so the fort was only for the use of the city's rulers.

ENDING THE WALK

Leave the Belvedere and turn left down Costa di San Giorgio, continuing on when this turns into Costa de' Magnoli, and, at Piazza Santa Maria Soprarno, turn left into Via de'Bardi. You are now at the southern end of the Ponte Vecchio. On your right, just before the bridge, is the **Golden View**, see ①④ – a good place for an *aperitivo*.

Above: on the church steps; admiring the view.

Food and Drink

③ FUORI PORTA
Via dei Monte Alle Croci 10r; tel: 055-234 2483; daily 12.30–3.30pm, 7pm–12.00am; €€
A little *enoteca* 'outside the gate' whose communal seating adds to the jovial atmosphere. The much-praised food is rustic and plentiful and consists of classic Tuscan dishes.

④ GOLDEN VIEW
Via de'Bardi 58r; tel: 055-214 502; daily noon–midnight; €€€
This attractive restaurant/pizzeria/*enoteca* overlooking the Arno is popular with tourists, especially at *aperitivo* time or when the live jazz strikes up. Cuisine is Tuscan with French and Mediterranean additions. Reservations are advised.

FIESOLE

This small village close to Florence, on the hills overlooking the city, has long attracted those in the city looking for a little peace away from the urban bustle and, during the summer, cooler air.

Culture Alfresco
The Teatro Romano is used for Fiesole's annual summer festival, Estate Fiesolana. For more details, *see p.122*.

DISTANCE 4km (2½ miles)
TIME A full day
START Piazza Mino
END Badia Fiesolana
POINTS TO NOTE

Buses from Florence to Fiesole run about three to four times an hour and the journey takes about 30 mins. The final stop is Fiesole Vinandro Osteria, close to Piazza Mino. Although you can get the bus back down again from Piazza Mino, it is far more pleasant to follow the route to the end, walking part of the way back down.

Fiesole is a favourite retreat for Florentines, who find the air in this hilltop village fresher than in the valley bottom, where their own city sits. Once, however, relations between the two places were not so comfortable. Fiesole predates Florence by some eight centuries; it was an Etruscan city well before the Romans colonised the area and founded the town from which Florence grew. Thereafter, Fiesole declined, but it remained an important trade competitor until 1125, when Florentine troops stormed it and destroyed all the buildings except for the cathedral.

From the 15th century onwards, numerous fine villas were built on the slopes leading up to Fiesole. Later, they were rented by a growing Anglo-Florentine community, which, in the 19th century, included the poets Robert and Elizabeth Barrett Browning.

TOWARDS PIAZZA MINO

You will see these villas from the bus as you approach Fiesole. To get there from central Florence, take bus no. 7 from Santa Maria Novella station or Piazza San Marco, buying your ticket from one of the ticket machines or cafés by the bus stop. The short journey from the city ends at the **Piazza Mino ❶**,

Food and Drink
① PIZZERIA ETRUSCA
Piazza Mino 2; tel: 055-599 484; Apr–Oct: daily 12.30–2.30pm and 6.30–10.30pm, Nov–Mar: Fri–Wed 12.30–2.30pm, 6.30–10.30pm; €
Set in the main piazza, this small *pizzeria* is a good place to grab a quick slice of something before heading off to explore.

Above from far left:
hilltop Fiesole;
the Teatro Romano
enjoys glorious views.

Fiesole's broad, main square, which occupies the site of the Roman forum. If you are peckish, drop into **Pizzeria Etrusca**, see ⑪①, to pick up a slice of pizza before carrying on.

ROMAN AMPHITHEATRE

From Piazza Mino head north across the square, to the right of the cathedral, to the entrance to the **Teatro Romano** and **Area Archeologica** ❷ (tel: 055-59477; Wed–Mon Apr–Sept 10am–7pm, Mar and Oct 10am–6pm, Nov–Feb 10am–2pm; charge, combination ticket includes Fiesole's other museums). The impeccably preserved amphitheatre, with a seating capacity of around 3,000, is the site of a popular arts festival held in July and August *(see p.122)*. It enjoys stunning views over the low, cypress-topped hills of the Mugello region to the north. Surrounding the theatre are the jumbled remains of Etruscan and Roman temples and baths. The excellent **Museo Archeologico**, in the same complex, displays tiny Etruscan figures (dancers, warriors, orators), sensual, headless statues of Dionysos and Venus and many other notable sculptures.

BANDINI MUSEUM

Almost directly opposite the entrance to the Teatro Romano, in Via Dupré, the **Museo Bandini** ❸ (same hours and ticket as the Teatro Romano) has an outstanding collection of paintings by the so-called Italian Primitives. This name was given to artists such as Taddeo and Agnolo Gaddi and Nardo di Cione,

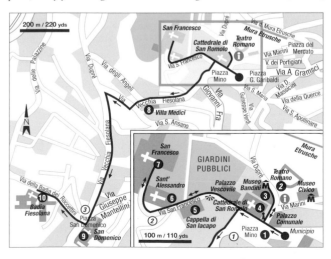

Above from left:
the arches of the
Teatro Romano;
summer flowers
in Fiesole.

who continued to work in the Gothic idiom well into the Renaissance era. Most of the paintings are religious, but there is an extremely rare and unusual late 15th-century allegorical work by Jacopo del Sellaio showing the *Triumph of Love, Time, Chastity and Piety.*

SAN ROMOLO CATHEDRAL

Head back to Piazza Mino, and, on your right, is the **Cattedrale di San Romolo** ❹ (tel: 055-599 566; daily, Apr–Oct: 7.30am–noon and 3–6pm, Nov–Mar: 7.30am–noon and 3–5pm; free). The apse of this severe, sandstone basilica contains 16th-century frescoes by local artist Nicodemo Ferrucci; they depict the life of St Romolo, whose sarcophagus is in the crypt below. The highlight of the church, however, is the tomb that Mino da Fiesole designed for the humanist Bishop Leonardo Salutati.

SAN IACAPO CHAPEL

Look for Via San Francesco, which climbs steeply opposite the cathedral façade. A short way up is the **Cappella di San Iacapo** ❺ (tel: 055-596 1293; currently closed for restoration, check www.cattedralefiesole.it for information), containing ecclesiastical treasures and early crucifixes. Further up, a terrace gives sweeping views over Florence.

SANT'ALESSANDRO

At the top of the lane is **Sant' Alessandro** ❻, whose plain, squat façade hides a 6th-century basilica with re-used Roman columns of green-veined *cipollino* (onion-ring) marble. It is the church of the friary of **San Francesco** ❼ (tel: 055-59175; Mon–Sat 9am–noon and 3–6pm, 5pm off season, Sun 3–6pm, 5pm off season; free) and was constructed on the site of an Etruscan temple.

It has been a monastery since the 15th century, and a monk will let you in to go upstairs and inspect the barren cells in which these holy men spent most of their lives. The church itself is packed with works of art, and, off the cloister, there is a curious museum full of dusty relics collected in China and Egypt by Franciscan missionaries.

It may now be time for lunch, and close by is **La Reggia degli Etruschi**, see ⑪②, with more great views (and lunch served from Thur–Sun).

Food and Drink 🍴

② LA REGGIA DEGLI ETRUSCHI
Via San Francesco 18; tel: 055-59385; Mon and Wed 7–10pm, Thur–Sun 1–2.30pm and 7–10pm; €€
The patio here offers a wonderful view over Florence spread out below. The food might not be quite as breathtaking as the view, but it's good, solid Italian fare nonetheless.

③ PIZZERIA SAN DOMENICO
Piazza San Domenico 11; tel: 055-59182; Tue–Sun noon–2.30pm and 6–10.30pm; €–€€
This is a simple restaurant with a huge selection of pizzas and pastas, and friendly service. Try one of the big salads followed by a *coppa della casa* (the house dessert).

BACK TO FLORENCE

You can now catch the bus back from Piazza Mino or walk part of the way, following the narrow Via Vecchia Fiesolana out of the square. En route you will pass the **Villa Medici** ❽ (tel: 800-414 2401; Mon–Fri 8.15am–6pm, 5pm off season, gardens only, by appointment at com.toscana@airc.it; charge), built in 1458, and a favourite retreat of Lorenzo de'Medici. Its gardens, and the view from its terraces are superb. On the descent, you can enjoy glimpses of other villas behind their high walls and note various examples of stonework and the typical Tuscan cypress trees.

The next stop on the route, after just 1km (0.5 mile), is the convent of **San Domenico** ❾ (tel: 055-59230; daily 9am–2pm and 5–8pm; free), home to

Fra Angelico's *Madonna with Angels* (1430) in the church and his *Crucifixion* (also from 1430) in the Chapter House.

From here, take the left fork down to the **Badia Fiesolana** ❿ (tel: 055-59155; Mon–Fri 9am–5pm, Sat 9am–noon; free), the church that served as Fiesole's cathedral until 1058. The original Romanesque façade, which is framed by the rough, unfinished stonework of the enlarged 15th-century church, is a delicate work of inlaid marble. There is another magnificent view over Florence from the terrace in front of the church.

Return to the Convent of San Domenico for the bus stop outside the church where the No. 7 bus will pick you up on the way back to Florence. If you fancy something to eat beforehand, then on Piazza San Domenico is the **Pizzeria San Domenico**, see ⑪③.

Recycled Motifs

The unfinished brick-and-stone façade of the Badia Fiesolana incorporates a green-and-white travertine and marble Romanesque façade of an earlier and smaller church.

Below: strolling through Fiesole.

MEDICI VILLAS

Not content with their sumptuous palaces and art works in Florence itself, the Medici built themselves beautiful residences in the countryside around the city. This tour visits two of the finest.

DISTANCE 2.5km (1½ miles)

TIME A full day

START Villa Corsini

END Villa Medicea Poggio ai Caiano

POINTS TO NOTE

Both villas are easily seen in one day (the Villa della Petraia in the morning and the Poggio ai Caiano in the afternoon), though each half of the tour could also be done separately. The gardens of the Villa della Petraia are lovely for a picnic; instead of eating back in town, you might want to pick up some edibles at the Mercato Centrale *(see p.52)* before you leave.

This tour is great for anyone with an interest in history and architecture, as well as garden-lovers, but do not expect colourful herbaceous borders: the two gardens to be visited were laid out in the formal Italian style in the 16th century and are of great historical interest. They can be enjoyed in all seasons. The garden of the Villa Medicea della Petraia is backed by extensive woodland, which is perfect for picnicking.

Catching the Bus

To reach them, take bus no. 2 or 28 from Via Luigi Alamanni, which runs down the western side of Santa Maria Novella railway station (see www.ataf.net). Buses leave around every 15 minutes, and tickets can be bought from the machine by the bus stop. The journey takes about 15 minutes, and, if possible, ask the driver to let you know where to get off for the Villa Medicea della Petraia. Alternatively, keep an eye on where you are going. The bus heads north to the suburb of Rifredi, then follows the railway track along the long Via Reginaldo Giuliani and the Via Sestese. Get off at stop 'Sestese 04'. Walk back a little way and turn left up Via Collodi; at the top turn right into Via Reginaldo Giuliani and then left up the narrow Via della Petraia.

VILLA CORSINI

About 500m (¼ mile) up the lane you will pass the **Villa Corsini ❶**, with its cream-coloured Baroque façade and a plaque recording that Robert Dudley died here on 6 September 1649. Dudley, the illegitimate son of the Earl of Leicester (Queen Elizabeth I's

favourite) was the leading marine engineer of his age and was employed by Cosimo I to build the harbour at Livorno (Tuscany's principal port).

Only the formal garden of the Villa Corsini is open to the public (Mon–Sat 9am–7pm). Laid out for Duke Cosimo I in 1541, it was once regarded as the supreme example of Renaissance gardening. The real point of your visit, however, lies a little further on.

VILLA MEDICEA DELLA PETRAIA

The **Villa Medicea della Petraia** ❷ (tel: 055-238 8717; www.polomuseale. firenze.it; daily, gardens: 8.15am–sunset; villa: by guided tour only every 45 mins from 8.30am, closed 2nd and 3rd Mon of the month; charge) is another 1km (½ mile) up from here. Enter the gate and take the first entrance in the wall on the right. You'll pass into the garden (laid out with flower beds enclosed by low box hedges)

that fronts the villa. Like many Italian gardens in the 18th century, these were designed in the style of English parkland. Take the central path up some steps and past a large fish pond to the terrace in front of the villa. From here the scroll work and geometric patterning of the box parterre can best be appreciated. There are also good views from here; left to the dome of Florence cathedral, straight ahead to the new industrial suburb of Firenze Nuova and right to the city's Peretola airport.

The Interior

Individual visitors can wander around the garden at will, but tours of the villa itself are only given to groups of 10, so you may have to wait and team up with other visitors (then press the bell to be let in). The main attraction inside is the central hallway, which is covered in frescoes detailing the history of the Medici. The villa was built in 1575 for Grand Duke Ferdinand I, on the site of an earlier fortress whose tower still stands.

Above from far left:
Villa Medicea della Petraia; historical painting *(The Clash)*, on the steps of the Villa Corsini.

Splendid Situation
The Villa Medicea della Petraia was built as a castle, then turned into a country mansion in the 1570s by Ferdinando de'Medici. It was altered again in the 19th century under the Savoys. One of its great features is its position, set out on a sloping hill.

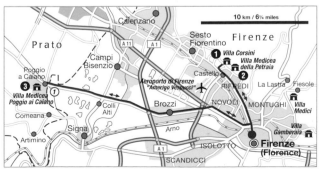

During the 19th century, Villa Medicea della Petraia was the favourite residence of the King of Italy, Victor Emmanuel II and it was he who had the tree house constructed in the huge (and now dead) ilex oak to the left of the villa's façade.

The Park

To the right of the villa, a gate in the wall leads to a large park full of ilex and cypress trees – offering cool respite even in the heat of summer – and threaded with little streams. This juxtaposition of the highly formal garden with wild and mysterious woodland was a favourite, and very effective, device of Italian gardeners from the Rennaissance onwards.

To return to Florence, retrace your steps to Via Sestese, cross the (usually busy) road and look for the bus stop down on the right (again bus no. 28 will take you back to Piazza Santa Maria Novella).

TO POGGIO AI CAIANO

Once back in Florence, you can either grab something to eat on Piazza Santa Maria Novella or at the Mercato Centrale or, if you have already had a picnic at Villa della Petraia, head straight off for the second of the two villas.

Below: magnificent gardens and views at the Villa Medicea della Petraia.

To reach Poggio ai Caiano, which is actually just over the boundary in the province of neighbouring Prato, 11 miles (18km) northwest of Florence, take one of the CAP buses from Santa Maria Novella (www.capautolinee.it). They depart every 25 minutes or so, and the journey takes about half an hour.

Villa Medicea Poggio ai Caiano

Alight at the stop on top of the small rise just outside the villa; either ask the driver to tell you when to get off, or keep a look out for the large walls enclosing the villa's gardens. This is the entrance to the **Villa Medicea Poggio ai Caiano ❸** (tel: 055-877 012; daily, gardens: 8.15am–sunset; villa: by guided tour only, hourly from 8.30am, closed 2nd and 3rd Mon of the month; free).

Often considered to be the 'most perfect' of the Medici's out-of-town residences, the villa has beautiful proportions. Its façade, by Sangallo, was modelled on a Greek temple on the instructions of Lorenzo the Magnificent. Above the main entrance, along the portico, is a glazed terracotta frieze by Andrea della Robbia.

The interior has been well restored. The highlights of the tour are the ground-floor private theatre, where the Medici were entertained by the leading actors of the day; and the large central hall upstairs with its superb frescoes.

The gardens are in two parts. To the front and side are the formal Italianate gardens with their large trees, carefully manicured flower beds and the lovely orangerie. Behind the villa is an attractive area of landscaped parkland, which is bounded by a small stream.

BACK TO FLORENCE

Once you have finished your tour of the villa and its gardens, then you have a choice: either take the bus straight back into town and find something to eat, or head just down the hill (back towards Florence). On the left is Piazza XX Settembre, where you can have an early dinner at **Il Falcone**, see ⑪①. This is ideal for a late lunch or early dinner after seeing the villa, but before sitting down to an evening meal first check the times of buses back to Florence.

Above from far left: interior and exterior of the Villa Medicea Poggio ai Caiano.

Food and Drink

① IL FALCONE

Piazza XX Settembre 35, Poggio a Caiano; tel: 055-877 065; Thur–Tue noon–2pm and 7–9.30pm; €€

This welcoming little restaurant dates back to the mid-19th century and has been in the same family for seven generations. It specialises in straightforward local dishes, such as *pappardelle* with goose, or wild boar, *ribollita* and excellent *trippa alla fiorentina*. One fish dish is served every Friday. The wine list offers a great selection of Chiantis and Super Tuscans.

SAN GIMIGNANO

This hilltop village, about halfway between Florence and Pisa, is one of Tuscany's most famous sights. Only 13 of the town's original 76 towers remain, but San Gimignano is still Italy's best-preserved medieval village.

DISTANCE 3km (2 miles)
TIME A full day
START Porta San Giovanni
END The Rocca
POINTS TO NOTE

This is an easy full-day excursion, which takes advantage of the efficient bus service. Arrive in San Gimignano as early as possible, before the tour buses (and accompanying crowds) arrive. Another option might be to stay overnight to see the village at its best during the evening and early morning.

Santa Fina

Off the south aisle of the Collegiata lies the Santa Fina Chapel, with Ghirlandaio's flowery depiction of the local saint. Legend has it that when she died in 1253, violets sprang up on her coffin and on the towers.

San Gimignano is a very popular excursion from Florence and easily reached by public transport. Take the Busitalia San Gimignano bus (the ticket office is at Via Santa Caterina da Siena 17r) from Santa Maria Novella station (www.fsbusitalia.it); it departs every hour and connects at Poggibonsi for another bus ride (www.trainspa.it) up to San Gimignano itself. The whole journey takes about 1½ hours, depending on the connection.

From Poggibonsi the approach is memorable, as the town's towers – the so-called *belle torri*, originally designed as keeps during the Guelf–Ghibelline feuds in the 12th and 13th centuries – come into view behind the olive trees, cypress trees and vines.

Arriving at **Porta San Giovanni ❶**, walk up Via San Giovanni to **Piazza della Cisterna ❷**. This lovely triangular square is named after its 13th-century well and lined with medieval *palazzi*. Also here is the **Gelateria di Piazza**, see 🍴①.

PIAZZA DEL DUOMO

Just beyond is the asymmetrical Piazza del Duomo, site of the **Palazzo del Popolo ❸** (tel: 0577-990 312; daily,

Mar–Oct: 9.30am–7pm, Nov–Feb: 10am–5pm; charge), with its 54-m (177ft) Torre Grossa, completed in around 1300. In the same square is the **Museo Civico** ❹ (same times and ticket as the Palazzo del Popolo) with an excellent collection of works by Florentine and Sienese masters, including pieces by Gozzoli, Lippi, Taddeo di Bartolo and Giotto.

On the far left-hand corner of the square is the Romanesque **Collegiata** (or **Duomo**) ❺ (tel: 0577-940316; Mar and Nov–Jan: Mon–Sat 10am–4.40pm, Sun 12.30–4.40pm, Apr–Oct: Mon–Fri 10am–7pm, Sat 10am–5.10pm, Sun 12.30–5.10pm; charge). Although this is the 'Duomo' after which the square is named, it no longer has the status of a cathedral because there is no resident bishop.

The plain façade belies the gloriously lavish interior; vaulted ceilings painted with gold stars, similar in style to Siena's Duomo *(see p.89)*, and walls covered in fine frescoes, mostly by Sienese artists. Look out for Bartolo di Fredi's vivid Old Testament scenes along the north aisle, and Barna di Siena's New Testament scenes covering the south wall. On the west wall are Benozzo Gozzoli's *Saint Sebastian* (c.1464) and Taddeo di Bartolo's gory *Last Judgement* (c.1393).

THE ROCCA

Continue on past the northern side of the Collegiata, turn left and then right, following a short road up to the **Rocca** ❻. This ruined 14th-century fortress offers a splendid view over the whole village as well as the surrounding countryside.

The bus back to Florence, again connecting at Poggibonsi, leaves from Porta San Giovanni so you will need to retrace your steps. From Mon–Sat the last bus is at 8.35pm and on Sundays at 8.20pm. On your way back down you might want to get an early dinner at **Dorandò**, see ⑪②.

Above from far left: San Gimignano 'skyscrapers'; rustic rooftops.

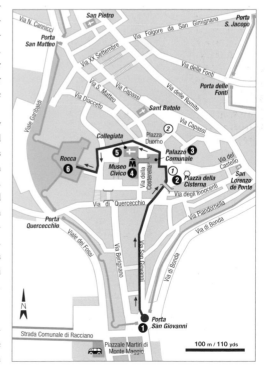

SIENA

This is a full day exploring the attractive medieval city of Siena, the arch-rival of Florence, with whom it fought many battles. Siena's art and architecture are superb – the glorious main square alone makes it worth a visit.

DISTANCE 1.5km (1 mile)
TIME A full day
START Il Campo
END Pinacoteca Nazionale
POINTS TO NOTE

Siena is a full day trip from Florence, but a relatively easy one, with the trains running late enough to allow for dinner in Siena.

City Layout

The city is divided into three districts or *terzi* (thirds) – the Terzo di Città, Terzo di San Martino and Terzo di Camollia. But this is purely admin-istrative: Siena's true identity is inextricably linked to the *contrade*, the 17 medieval districts from which its social fabric is woven.

Food and Drink

① AL MANGIA
Il Campo 42; tel: 0577-47093; daily 12.30–2.30pm, 7–10.30pm; €€€–€€€€
In a wonderful position on the Campo, this restaurant serves good classic Tuscan cuisine, and is popular with tourists and locals alike. Outside tables are available in summer. You pay a premium for the location, but it is worth it.

② OSTERIA IL CARROCCIO
Via Casato di Sotto 32; tel: 0577-41165; Thur–Tue noon–2.30pm and 7–10.30pm; €
A well-run, quaint and tiny *trattoria* serving simple local dishes not far from the Campo. Friendly and cosy. Outdoor dining available.

According to legend, the city of Siena was founded by Senius, son of Remus; hence the she-wolf symbols seen around the city. There is a long history – starting in the 12th century – of rivalry between the (usually triumphant) Florentine Guelfs and the Sienese Ghibellines. Everywhere there are reminders of this longstanding enmity, both in Siena and in the strategically placed fortified towns scattered throughout its province.

Arrival

Trains leave from Santa Maria Novella every hour (www.fsitaliane.it), with the journey lasting 90 minutes and last train returning at 9.27pm. The bus can be faster: Busitalia coaches (www.fsbus italia.it) leave every 30 minutes in high season. The trip takes 75 minutes. From the train station, take a local bus (nos 3 or 10; www.siena mobilita.it) for the 10-minute journey to Via Tozzi (Busitalia buses stop here), then walk down Via Montanini and Via Bianchi di Sopra to reach **Il Campo ❶**, Siena's main square.

IL CAMPO

This beautiful space – Il Campo, or Piazza del Campo – spreads out from

the Gothic town hall like a fan, with the Fonte Gaia fountain at its tip. Cobblestones divide the piazza into nine segments, meant to represent the Governo dei Nove (Council of the Nine), an oligarchy of merchants who ruled the medieval city until the end of its golden age in 1355. It was during their rule that the finest works of Sienese art and architecture were commissioned or completed, including the Campo and the **Palazzo Pubblico ❷**.

PALAZZO PUBBLICO

Considered to be one of the most beautiful Gothic buildings in Tuscany, this *palazzo* contains the **Museo Civico** (tel: 0577-530 164; daily Oct–mid Mar 10am–6pm, mid Mar–Sep: to 7pm; charge), which is more a fabulously decorated palace than a classic museum. The main council chamber is adorned with Simone Martini's *Maestà* – depicting the Madonna on a filigree throne – and his celebrated fresco of a *condottiere* (mercenary).

For a glorious view of the piazza and the rooftops, climb the **Torre del Mangia** but be prepared to queue. At 102m (335ft) the belltower is the second highest in Italy. The **Cappella in Piazza** (Chapel in the Square) at the bottom of the tower was erected in 1378 in thanksgiving for the end of the plague. You will find the statue of the Mangia, the gluttonous bellringer that the tower is named after, in the Cor-

tile del Podestà, the courtyard that lies next to the chapel. Before carrying on, you might like to eat on the square at **Al Mangia**, see ⑪①, or just behind it at **Osteria Il Carroccio**, see ⑪②.

THE DUOMO

From the Campo, head south past the Palazzo Chigi-Saracini and then turn immediately right and then left into Via di Città.

Carry on to the next turning on the right and walk straight down to Siena's wonderful cathedral, the **Duomo ❸** (tel: 0577-286 300; www.operaduomo. siena.it; Mar–Nov 10.30am–7pm, Nov–Feb 10.30am–5.30pm; charge).

Above from far left: Palazzo Pubblico; Il Campo during the biennial Palio.

The Palio

Siena's famous horse race, the Palio, takes place twice annually and lasts just 90 seconds but it is the highlight of the year for many of the city's inhabitants. The Palio (www.ilpalio.org) has been held since the 13th century, when the August Palio made its debut. At that time, the contest took the form of a bareback race the length of the city. The race run around Siena's main square, the Piazza del Campo, was introduced in the 17th century and today takes place on 2 July and 16 August. The costume parade, which is staged in the run-up to the main race, retraces Siena's centuries of struggle against Florence, from the glorious victory against its arch-rival in 1260 to the ghastly defeat in 1560. The race then begins and hurtles around the Campo three times. If a riderless horse wins, the animal is almost deified: it is given the place of honour in the victory banquet and has its hooves painted gold.

Above from left:
clock of the Palazzo Pubblico; rooftop view of Siena; the distinctive zebra stripes of the Duomo.

Above: local cakes.

Part riotous Gothic and part austere Romanesque, the Duomo is perched on one of Siena's three hills. The interior is an equally dazzling mix of styles with its soaring black-and-white pillars and inlaid marble floors. The exquisite pulpit was carved by Niccolò Pisano and the Libreria Piccolomini holds the illuminated manuscripts of Pope Pius II. The frescoes by Pinturicchio (1509) depict scenes from the life of the influential Renaissance pope, a member of the noble Sienese Piccolomini family and founder of Renaissance Pienza.

Cathedral Museum

In the eastern section of the Duomo, unfinished because of the Black Death, is the **Museo dell'Opera del Duomo ❹** (tel: 0577-283 048; www.opera duomo.siena.it; same hours as Duomo; charge). The museum is famed for its marble statues carved by Giovanni Pisano for the façade, and for Duccio's altarpiece of *The Virgin and Child Enthroned in Majesty*, or *Maestà* (1308–11, *see margin*).

Baptistry

Continuing on around the northern edge of the Duomo to Piazza San Giovanni brings you to the **Battistero San Giovanni ❺** (daily, 9.30am-7.30pm, 5.30pm off season; charge). Built in 1316–25, the Baptistry has a tall Gothic façade. The superb interior is adorned with frescoes by, among others, Lorenzo di Pietro (Vecchietta). The font (1431) has gilded bronze bas-reliefs by Jacopo della Quercia, Donatello and Ghiberti.

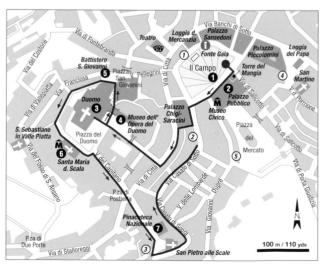

SANTA MARIA DELLA SCALA

On the far side of the Duomo the **Santa Maria della Scala** ❻ (tel: 0577-534 571; mid-Mar–mid-Oct 10.30am–6.30pm, mid-Oct–mid-Mar 10.30am–4.30pm, last entry 30 mins before closing; www.santamariadella scala.com; charge) is the former pilgrims' hospital, in its heyday one of the most important hospitals in the world. Much of the vast complex has been restored and turned into a cultural centre. The main ward, the Sala Pellegrinaio, boasts stunning frescoes by Domenico di Bartolo narrating the history of the hospital. The old hayloft or *fienile* now houses Jacopo della Quercia's original sculpted panels from the *Fonte Gaia* (Fountain of Joy) in Siena's Campo. Other highlights are the Oratorio di Santa Caterina della Notte, the Church of Santissima Annunziata and the city's architectural museum with a great collection of Etruscan remains.

PINACOTECA NAZIONALE

Take Via del Capitano south from the piazza. About 200m/yds further on is the **Pinacoteca Nazionale** ❼ (National Gallery; tel: 577-281 161; Tue–Sat 9am 5.15pm, Sun–Mon 9am–1pm; charge). This collection, housed in the suitably Gothic Palazzo Buonsignori, holds great works of art from the Siena School, famed for its *fondi d'oro*: paintings with lavish, gilded backgrounds.

From here it is easy to head back to Il Campo along Via Casato di Sopra. Good places to eat in the vicinity include the **Osteria del Castelvecchio**, see ⑪③, **Le Logge**, see ⑪④, and the **Trattoria Papei**, see ⑪⑤.

The *Maestà*

Siena's best-loved work of art, the *Maestà*, is kept in the Duomo's Sala il Duccio, a dramatically lit room that sets off to perfection one of the most important paintings in medieval art. The *Maestà* was completed in 1311 and escorted from the artist's workshop to the Duomo in a torchlit procession; the double-sided panel painting graced the High Altar until 1506.

Food and Drink

③ OSTERIA DEL CASTELVECCHIO
Via Castelvecchio 65; tel: 0577-47093; Wed–Mon noon–2.30pm and 7–10.30pm; €€
Converted from ancient stables, this lovely informal *osteria* serves traditional and often lesser-known Sienese dishes. There are good daily choices for vegetarians and lots of excellent meat dishes, plus an interesting wine list. Opening times tend to change, so check when you book.

④ OSTERIA LE LOGGE
Via del Porrione 33; tel: 0577-48013; Mon–Sat noon–2.45pm and 7–10.30pm; €€–€€€
This restaurant is set in a 19th-century grocer's shop with an authentic dark-wood and marble interior. The menu is likely to offer duck and fennel, pasta with black truffles and stuffed guinea fowl (*faraona*).

⑤ TRATTORIA PAPEI
Piazza del Mercato 6; tel: 0577-280 894; Tue–Sun noon–3pm and 7–10.30pm; €€
This is an ideal place for Sienese home cooking, such as *pappardelle al sugo di cinghiale* (pasta in wild boar sauce) or *pici alla cardinale* (pasta in a hot tomato sauce with *pancetta*), as well as good grilled meat plates.

PISA

This easy excursion from Florence takes in Pisa's essential sights. The crowds of tourists are inevitable, but do not detract too much from the enjoyment of the world-famous Leaning Tower, cathedral, Baptistry and Camposanto.

'Universalis'
This is the name of the ticket, valid for 8 days and issued by the Pisa Commune, that for only €13 gives access to 10 museums and churches, including some of those in this tour. Of these, however, only Santa Maria della Spina *(see p.97)* or the Museo delle Sinopie *(see p.96)* sell the Universalis, so you will need to head to either of these first and then retrace your route to visit.

DISTANCE 5km (3 miles)
TIME A full day
START Piazza dei Cavalieri
END Santa Maria della Spina
POINTS TO NOTE

The best way to get to Pisa is by train. Trains run regularly from Santa Maria Novella station (see www.trenitalia.com for times) and fares are cheap. Be prepared for long queues at the Leaning Tower. You can reserve tickets 15–45 days in advance at www.opapisa.it for an extra €2. Children under 8 are not allowed up the tower and those aged 8–18 must be accompanied by an adult.

Many visitors to Florence arrive and depart from Pisa's Galileo Galilei airport, but do not find time to visit Pisa itself. This is a pity, since it is very easy to reach from Florence, and its sights are memorable.

Trains depart from Santa Maria Novella station in Florence roughly every half hour and the journey takes just over an hour. The train follows the Arno valley downstream, calling first at the industrial town of Empoli, before arriving at Pisa Centrale station.

To the Arno

Leave the station, head straight up Viale Gramsci, crossing the busy Piazza Vittorio Emanuele and continuing up Corso Italia. This brings you to the banks of the River Arno, which is much wider here than in Florence. Cross the Ponte di Mezzo to Piazza Garibaldi and walk up the arcaded Borgo Stretto, Pisa's animated main shopping street. Take the first left, Via Ulisse Dini, to reach the **Piazza dei Cavalieri** ❶ (Square of the Knights).

PIAZZA DEI CAVALIERI

This square is dominated by the Palazzo della Carovana, built by Vasari in 1562 and covered in black-and-white sgraffito decoration, featuring signs of the Zodiac and mythical figures. The *palazzo* (now a high school) stands on the site of Pisa's original *municipio* (town hall), which was demolished in 1509 to symbolise the subjugation of Pisa after the city had been defeated by the powerful Florentines.

Santa Stefano

A large statue of Duke Cosimo I stands in front of the palace. To the right, the church of **Santo Stefano della Cavalieri ❷** (tel: 050-580 814; Oct–Mar: Mon–Sat 11am–4.30pm, Sun 11.30am–5.30pm, Apr–Sept: daily 10am–7pm; charge) holds war trophies captured by the crusading *cavalieri* (knights) of St Stephen in battles against the Turks.

Above from far left: the Duomo; the famous tower, with cherub statue.

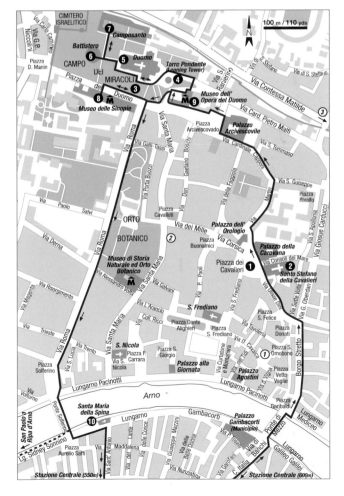

Above from left: rising tiers of colonnades decorate the Duomo; quirky Pisan postbox.

Just to the left is the **Palazzo dell' Orologio** (Palace of the Clock), which incorporates the grim **Torre Gualandi**, known as the Tower of Hunger. This is where Count Ugolino, along with all his sons and grandsons, was walled up and starved to death in 1288 for allegedly betraying Pisa to the Genoese. The tragic story is told both in Dante's *Inferno* (Canto xxxiii) and in Percy Bysshe Shelley's 1820 poem, *The Tower of Famine*.

A few streets from the square is a good place for something to eat: the **Trattoria Sant'Omobono**, see ⑪①.

FIELD OF MIRACLES

Pass under the arch beneath the clock tower and take the right-hand street, Via Martiri. This bends left to join Via Cardinale Capponi, which leads to the **Campo dei Miracoli ❸** (Field of Miracles), where the famous ensemble of Pisa's Torre Pendente (Leaning Tower), the cathedral and the Baptistry is revealed. No matter how many photographs you may have seen, nothing prepares you for the impact of these extraordinary buildings when seen at first hand.

Pisa was a thriving port (until the mouth of the Arno silted up in the 16th century), and the city had extensive trade contacts with Spain and North Africa during the 12th and 13th centuries. This explains the Moorish influence on the architecture of these buildings, which is evident in the marble arabesque patterns that cover the walls of the cathedral and the bristling, minaret-like pinnacles of the Baptistry. All of the buildings tilt (because of badly built foundations), not just the Leaning Tower, so you may experience sensations of vertigo if you look at them for too long.

The ticket office for these buildings is to the right, beside the Leaning Tower. Various combinations are on offer, depending on which monuments you want to visit, including a good-value, all-inclusive ticket.

LEANING TOWER

The **Torre Pendente ❹** (tel: 050-835 011; www.opapisa.it; daily Jan and Dec 10am–4.30pm, Feb and Nov 9.30am–5.30pm, Mar 9am–5.30pm, Oct 9am–7pm; Apr–Sept 8.30am–8pm; 30 minute guided tours; tickets from ticket office behind tower or Museo delle Sinopie on south side of the Campo dei Miracoli: charge), begun in 1173, started to tilt during the early stages of construction, when it was only 10.5m (35ft) high. Some people like to joke that the Pisans deliberately built it this way, so as to ensure a healthy income from tourism in years to come. Completed in 1350, the tower has continued to slide, and now, at 54.5m (180ft) high, it leans 4.5m (15ft) from the perpendicular. An ambitious 10-year underpinning pro-

gramme has stabilised the tower and visitors are once again allowed to climb it. Forty people are permitted to climb the 294 steps every 30 minutes.

THE DUOMO

The **Duomo** ❺ (Cathedral; tel: 050-835 011; www.opapisa.it; Nov–Feb: daily 10am–1pm and 2–5pm, Mar 10am–6pm, Oct 10am–7pm, Apr–Sept 10am–8pm; charge) alongside the tower is as interesting for its exterior as its interior. It was begun in 1063, and the façade is covered in rising tiers of colonnades that are typical of the distinctive Pisan Romanesque style. The bronze doors below date from 1602 and illustrate various biblical scenes. The cathedral is entered through the south transept, which also has important Romanesque bronze doors, designed by Bonnano da Pisa in 1180; these illustrate scenes from the Life of Christ.

The Interior
Fire devastated the interior in 1595 but spared Cimabue's mosaic of *Christ in Majesty* (1302) in the vault of the apse and the outstanding pulpit, carved with New Testament scenes. This is the work of the father-and-son team, Niccolò and Giovanni Pisano. Although it dates from the 13th century, when Gothic was the predominant style, their style anticipates the best Renaissance sculpture of the following century.

BAPTISTRY

You will see more proto-Renaissance sculpture in the **Battistero** ❻ (tel: 050-835 011; daily, Nov–Feb: 10am–5pm, Mar: 9am–6pm, Apr–Sept: 8am–8pm, Oct: 9am–7pm; charge). The Baptistry was designed and completed by the Pisani in 1284 and contains Niccolò Pisano's first important work, the fine pulpit with panels carved with animated scenes from the Life of Christ.

HOLY FIELD

Giorgio Vasari, the great 16th-century art historian, informs us that the Pisani were influenced by the carvings on the Roman sarcophagi that are to be found in the **Camposanto** ❼ (Holy Field; tel: 050-560 547; daily, Nov–Feb 9am–4.30pm, Mar and Oct 9am–5.30pm, April–Sept 8am–7.30pm; charge), the cemetery that lies to the north of the cathedral and is enclosed by marble walls. This was

Sacred Shape
Buscheto, the original architect of the Duomo, combined the ground plan of an early Christian basilica with a transept, making this the first sacred building built in the shape of a cross in Italy.

Food and Drink 🍴

① TRATTORIA SANT'OMOBONO
Piazza Sant'Omobono 6; tel: 050-540 847; Mon–Sat 12.30–2.30pm and 7.30–10pm; €€
This decent little restaurant, not far from Piazza dei Cavalieri, serves good local food. Among the dishes are roast pork, salt cod and pasta with local sausage. The interior has a nicely antique feel, and the service is friendly.

Pisan Regatta

In mid-June Pisa holds its Regatta di San Ranieri, when boat races and processions of decorated boats are held on the River Arno. The evening before the regatta, tens of thousands of candles and torches are placed on the buildings along the river.

Below: fresh pesto and *tagliatelle*.

begun in 1278, and shiploads of soil were brought back from the Holy Land in Pisan ships, along with the sarcophagi, to add sanctity to the burial ground.

The cloister walls around the cemetery were once gloriously frescoed, but they were damaged when a stray Allied bomb hit the cemetery in 1944. Even so, fragments remain of a lively Last Judgment by an unknown 14th-century artist.

Before carrying on to the nearby museums you may want some lunch. Two options just a short walk away are the **Osteria i Santi**, see ⑪②, and the **Antica Trattoria da Bruno**, see ⑪③.

PISAN MUSEUMS

On the south side of the Campo dei Miracoli is the **Museo delle Sinopie** ❽ (tel: 050-560 547; daily, Nov–Feb 9am–4.30pm, Mar and Oct: 9am–5.30pm, Apr–Sept: 8am–7.30pm; charge), which is where the remaining frescoes from the Camposanto are on display. Many consist of nothing more than the *sinopie*, the preliminary designs sketched into the plaster undercoat to guide the artist during the final stage, when the finished fresco is painted onto the moist final coat of plaster.

Also of interest is the **Museo dell'Opera del Duomo** ❾ (tel: 050-560

547; daily, Nov–Feb 9am–4.30pm, Mar and Oct 9am–5.30pm, Apr–Sept: 8am–7.30pm; charge) on the corner of the Piazza del Duomo nearest to the Leaning Tower. This museum contains numerous works of art, including Giovanni Pisano's exquisite ivory *Virgin and Child*. The museum's courtyard also offers an unusual view of the Leaning Tower.

ROMANESQUE AND GOTHIC CHURCHES

You can retrace your steps back to the station from here if you want to go straight back to Florence, or extend the route via two churches with exceptional exterior decoration. From Piazza del Duomo, take Via Roma southwards, passing the **Orto Botanico** (Botanical Garden) on your left until you reach the Arno embankment.

At this point, you could cross over the Ponte Solferino and turn right along Lungarno Sidney Sonnino to reach the church of **San Paolo a Ripa d'Arno**, which has a fine Pisan Romanesque façade. For the main walk, however, turn left into Lungarno Gambacorti after the bridge, towards **Santa Maria della Spina** ❿ (tel: 055-321 5446; Nov–Feb: Tue–Sun 10am–2pm, every 2nd Sun of the month 10am–7pm, Mar–Oct: Tue–Fri 10am–1.30pm and 2.30–6pm, Sat–Sun 10am–1.30pm and 2.30–7pm; charge). This 14th-century

Gothic church was built to house a single thorn from Christ's Crown of Thorns; a theme that is picked up by the bristling exterior, covered with prickly pinnacles and niches containing statues of Christ, the Virgin and the Apostles, and gives the church its name.

A right turn after the church will take you down Via Sant'Antonio and back to Pisa Centrale station, from where you can take the train back to Florence.

Above: along the Arno in Pisa.

Food and Drink
② OSTERIA I SANTI
Via Santa Maria 71; tel: 050-28081; daily 12.30–2.30pm, 7–10.30pm; €
Away from the tourist traps around the Campo dei Miracoli, this family-run restaurant is about a 10-minute walk away to the south. The food comprises simple, straightforward Tuscan dishes that are perfectly adequate and very reasonably priced.

③ ANTICA TRATTORIA DA BRUNO
Via Luigi Bianchi 12; tel: 050-560 818; Wed–Sun noon–3pm, 7–10.30pm; €€
Again, some 10 minutes' walk away east from the monuments but worth the detour, this well-established *trattoria* is a good place for lunch or an early dinner. It offers a good range of local dishes, including salt cod with leeks, pasta with chick peas and *zuppa pisana*.

DIRECTORY

A user-friendly alphabetical listing of practical information, plus hand-picked hotels and restaurants, clearly organised by area, to suit all budgets and tastes. Select nightlife listings are also included here.

A

AGE RESTRICTIONS

The age of consent for heterosexual, gay and lesbian sex is 14. You must be 18 to drive and 16 to buy alcohol.

B

BUDGETING

Florence is relatively expensive in terms of accommodation with little under €100 per night at the budget end of things, and the sky being the limit for the luxury hotels. Depending on what wine you choose, a glass will cost around €4–6. Allow €25-40 per head for an evening meal.

A standard bus fare is €1.20 for 90 minutes of travel. A 24-hour ticket is €5, and a three-day pass costs €12.

The Firenze Card is a museum and public transport pass (€50) which is valid for 72 hours and allows admission to 50 museums (including the famous ones) in Florence and the area plus unlimited travel on public transport. This represents good value for keen sightseers and it means skipping the queues, but if you are just visiting a couple of museums, it is not worth the outlay. Under the new Martedi in Arte initiative the major state museums are free to the public from 7–11pm on the last Tuesday of every month.

C

CHILDREN

At first sight, art- and architecture-heavy Florence may not appear to be the best place to take children, but there are some museums and other sights that hold some appeal (such as climbing the dome of the Duomo or the mummies in the Museo Archaeologico). The Boboli Garden and the Cascine are Florence's two main parks, where kids can let off steam, while one of the few children's playgrounds is to be found in Piazza dell'Azeglio. Italians are very fond and tolerant of children, and finding a restaurant to eat with them should not be a problem. Florence also has numerous ice cream parlours, which should be popular with kids.

CLOTHING

Casual wear is acceptable in all but the grandest restaurants. Clothing should be as light as possible for summer, but take a jumper for the evenings, which can be surprisingly cool. If you go in spring or autumn, it is worth taking a light raincoat or umbrella. In winter (Nov–Mar), the temperature frequently drops to freezing or below, and warm clothing is essential. A pair of comfortable shoes is invaluable for sightseeing and walking the cobbled streets. Shorts and bare shoulders are frowned upon and frequently forbidden in churches.

CUSTOMS AND DUTY-FREE

It is no longer possible to buy duty-free or tax-free goods on journeys within the European Union (EU). VAT and duty are included in the purchase price. Shops at ports and airport terminals will sell goods duty- and tax-paid to those travelling within the EU; they may choose not to pass on price increases. Airports can have separate duty-free shops for those travelling outside the EU or single shops selling duty-free goods alongside duty-/tax-paid goods.

Since the sale of duty-free goods in any EU country has been abolished, there are no longer any limits on how much you can buy on journeys within the EU, provided it is for your own personal use. However, there are certain suggested limits, and if you exceed them, the customs department may seize your goods if you cannot prove they are for your own use. The guidance levels are 800 cigarettes or 400 cigarillos or 200 cigars or 1kg of smoking tobacco; 10 litres of spirits; 20 litres of fortified wine; 90 litres of wine; 110 litres of beer. Duty-free is still available to those travelling outside the EU.

D

DISABLED TRAVELLERS

Despite difficult cobbled streets and poor wheelchair access to tourist attractions and hotels, many people with disabilities visit Florence and Tuscany every year. Unaccompanied visitors will usually experience some difficulty, so it is best to travel with a companion. Specialised tour operators or travel agencies offering customised tours and itineraries for those with disabilities include Flying Wheels Travel (www.flyingwheels travel.com) and Accessible Journeys (www.disabilitytravel.com). Access-Able Travel Source (www.access-able.com) is a database of travel agents from around the world with experience in accessible travel. In the UK you can obtain further information from RADAR (www.radar.org.uk) and in the US from SATH (www.sath.org).

E

ELECTRICITY

Italy uses 220v and two-pin plugs, for which you will need an adaptor.

EMBASSIES AND CONSULATES

Australian Embassy: Via Antonio Bosio 5, 00161 Rome; tel: 06-852 721.
UK Embassy: Via XX Settembre 80a, 00187 Rome; tel: 06-4220 0001.
UK Consulate: Lungarno Corsini 2, 50123 Florence; tel: 055-284 133.
US Embassy: Via Vittorio Veneto 121, 00187 Rome; tel: 06-46741.
US Consulate: Lungarno A. Vespucci 38, 50123 Florence; tel: 055-266 951.

Above from far left: Tuscan blooms; carved wooden Pinocchios in a traditional toy shop.

Crime and Safety
While Florence is generally a safe city, petty crime is a major problem, particularly pick-pocketing and the snatching of handbags and jewellery in the street and on buses. One popular scam is for someone to approach you to distract your attention while someone else steals your purse or wallet. Keep your valuables hidden on your person and your hand on your bag to help avoid this. Make sure you report any thefts to the police, since you will need evidence of the crime in the form of a police report to claim insurance.

EMERGENCIES

Police *(Carabinieri)*: 112
Police *(Polizia)*: 113
Fire Brigade *(Vigili del Fuoco)*: 115
Ambulance *(Misericordia)*: 118
Tourist Police: tel: 055-203 911

Etiquette
Italians tend to be friendly, but will have no qualms about showing their displeasure should you do something to offend them. Being polite and trying to speak a little Italian goes a long way. Both men and women greet each other with a kiss on each cheek.

F

FESTIVALS

Easter Day: *Scoppio del Carro*, the Explosion of the Cart (actually fireworks on a float). An ancient ritual accompanied by processions of musicians and flag-throwers in Renaissance costume, starting at the Porta a Prato and ending at Piazza del Duomo.

Ascension Day: *Festa del Grillo*, Festival of the Crickets, in Parco delle Cascine. Children used to bring or buy crickets in cages, but the insects have now been replaced by toy versions. There's also a large general market.

End of April: *Flower Show*, in the Parterre, near Piazza della Libertà.

May and June: *Maggio Musicale Fiorentino*. A festival comprising opera, ballet, concerts and recitals. It closes with two free concerts held in the Piazza della Signoria.

16–17 June: *Luminaria di San Ranieri* (Pisa). A spectacular event, with thousands of candles lit on the buildings along the Arno. A boat race takes place on the second day.

24 June: *San Giovanni*. Florence's patron saint's day and a public holiday in the city. The *calcio* in costume football game is played in Piazza Santa Croce; other matches are also played around this time.

Last Sunday in June: *Il Gioco del Ponte* (Pisa). A kind of medieval tug-of-war played out on the Ponte di Mezzo.

2 July and 16 August: Palio horse races (Siena). The famous horse races take place on these two dates.

July: *Florence Dance Festival*. A three-week festival of dance at outdoor venues in Florence.

FURTHER READING

Art and Architecture
The Architecture of the Italian Renaissance. Peter Murray (Schocken, 1997). Originally published in 1967, this volume by a professor of Birkbeck College, London, remains the classic guide to the art and architecture of the Renaissance period.

Autobiography. Benvenuto Cellini (Penguin Classics, 1999). The troubled life of the Florentine artist gives valuable insight into life during the Renaissance period.

Italian Architecture from Michelangelo to Borromini. Antony Hopkins (Thames & Hudson, 2002). Tracking the artistic period from the High Renaissance through Mannerism to Baroque, this book helps explain the background to much of Florence's artistic patrimony.

Lives of the Artists: Volumes 1 and 2. Giorgio Vasari (Oxford World's Classics, 2008). An entertaining and biased account of the lives of many important figures in Florentine art by the 16th-century architect and artist.

Culture and History

The Civilisation of the Renaissance in Italy. Jacob Burckhardt (Penguin, 1990). Published in 1860, this was a defining work in the study of the Italian Renaissance. It remains an illuminating account of the myriad artistic, scientific and philosophical developments of the era.

Florence: The Biography of a City. Christopher Hibbert (Penguin, 1994). This book weaves together the history and culture of Florence, with photographs and illustrations to make the narrative come to life.

The Rise and Fall of the House of Medici. Christopher Hibbert (Penguin, 1979). This witty insight into the dynasty that ruled Florence is by an author who has written extensively on the city.

Literature

A Room with a View. E.M. Forster (Penguin Classics, 2000). Forster's classic novel and social study of class and the mores of the English holidaying in Florence in the Edwardian period.

Love and War in the Apennines. Eric Newby (Hodder & Stoughton, 1971). A story of the escape of a British prisoner of war in Italy in World War II.

The Prince. Niccolò Machiavelli (Penguin 2003). Machiavelli's classic treatise on power in the Renaissance.

A Traveller's Companion to Florence. Harold Acton and Edward Chaney, Eds (Robinson Publishing 2002). An overview of Florence, based on letters and memoirs from several renowned Florentine ex-pat personalities.

G

GAY AND LESBIAN TRAVELLERS

Florence is an easy-going destination for gay and lesbian visitors, with a lively local scene helped by the presence of many students and the Florentines' generally liberal outlook on life. The national LGBT organisation Arcigay (tel: 055-012 3121; www. Arcigay.it) has an active branch in the city (Via di Mezzo 39r) that can provide help and information. Their website (in Italian only) features useful information on local activism and events.

GREEN ISSUES

The mayor of Florence is giving high priority to eco-friendly transport, reducing smog and preserving green areas of the city. His first move was to ban all vehicles from the city centre which will substantially reduce the carbon monoxide and fine partic-

ulate that was suffocating the city centre – and sullying the Duomo. Small electric buses weave their way around the periphery, and there are an increasing number of bike lanes. However, outlying streets are clogged with traffic and you will see many cars parked on pavements.

H

HEALTH

Insurance
EU residents are entitled to the same medical treatment as an Italian citizen. Visitors will need to get an EHIC card (see www.ehic.org.uk for information) before they go. This covers medical treatment and medicines, although it is still necessary to pay prescription charges and a percentage of the costs for medicines. Note that the EHIC does not give any cover for trip cancellations, nor does it provide repatriation in case of illness. For this, you will need to take out private insurance. Canadian citizens are also covered by a reciprocal arrangement between the Italian and Canadian governments. US citizens, however, are strongly advised to take out private health insurance.

If you are covered by a reciprocal scheme and need to visit a doctor while in Italy, take the EHIC card (if an EU resident) or proof of citizenship and residence (eg passport) to the local health office (Unità Sanitaria Locale), which will direct you to a doctor covered by the state system and supply the necessary paperwork.

Pharmacies and Hospitals
Pharmacies: the staff in chemists' shops *(farmacie)* are usually very knowledgeable about common illnesses and sell far more medicines without prescription than their colleagues in other Western countries.

Every *farmacia* has a list of the local pharmacies which are open at night and on Sundays.

Chemists' shops that are open 24 hours *(farmacie aperte 24 ore su 24)* in Florence are:
Farmacia Comunale, Santa Maria Novella Station; tel: 055-216 761.
Farmacia Molteni, Via dei Calzaiuoli 7r; tel: 055-215 472.

There is an accident and emergency department in the city centre at Ospedale Santa Maria Nuova, Piazza Santa Maria Nuova 1; tel: 055-69381.

HOURS AND HOLIDAYS

Business Hours
Offices are usually open from 8am–1pm and from 2–4pm, though many now stay open all day. Normal banking hours are Mon–Fri 8.30am–noon and 2.30–4.30pm. On national holidays, all shops, offices and schools are closed. Standard shop opening times

are Mon–Sat 8.30/9am to 1/1.30pm and 3.30/4pm to 7.30/8pm but an increasing number of shops are open all day.

Public Holidays

The dates of the national holidays in Florence are:

1 Jan *Capodanno* (New Year's Day)

Easter *Pasqua*

Easter Monday *Pasquetta*

25 Apr *Anniversario della Liberazione* (Liberation Day)

1 May *Festa del Lavoro* (Workers' Day)

24 June *San Giovanni* (St John the Baptist, Florence's patron saint)

15 Aug *Ferragosti* (Assumption of the Blessed Virgin Mary)

1 Nov *Tutti Santi* (All Saints' Day)

8 Dec *Immacolata Concezione* (Immaculate Conception)

25 Dec *Natale* (Christmas)

26 Dec *Santo Stefano* (Boxing Day)

L

LANGUAGE

Basic Italian

Yes *Sì*

No *No*

Hello *Salve*

Thank you *Grazie*

Yes please *Sì grazie*

Many thanks *Mille grazie/tante grazie/ molte grazie*

You're welcome *Prego*

All right/OK/That's fine *Va bene*

Please *Per favore* or *per cortesia*

Excuse me (to get attention) *Scusi* (singular), *Scusate* (plural)

Excuse me (to get through a crowd) *Permesso*

Wait a minute! *Aspetta!*

Could you help me? (formal) *Potrebbe aiutarmi?*

Certainly *Ma, certo*

Can I help you? (formal) *Posso aiutarla?*

Can you help me? *Può aiutarmi, per cortesia?*

I need… *Ho bisogno di…*

Can you show me…? *Può indicarmi…?*

I'm lost *Mi sono perso*

I'm sorry *Mi dispiace*

I don't know *Non lo so*

I don't understand *Non capisco*

Do you speak English? *Parla inglese?*

Could you speak more slowly, please? *Può parlare piu lentamente, per favore?*

Could you repeat that please? *Può ripetere, per favore?*

slowly/quietly *piano*

here/there *qui/là*

What? *Quale/come?*

When/why/where? *Quando/perchè/dove?*

Where is the toilet? *Dov'è il bagno?*

open/close *aperto/chiuso*

pull/push *tirare/spingere*

LEFT LUGGAGE

Left-luggage facilities can be found at Santa Maria Novella railway station.

Above from far left: olive tree; architectural detail.

Internet and Email Many hotels offer internet access and WiFi, and there are plenty of internet cafés open until late. The Florence WiFi initiative provides free one-hour internet access in 26 locations around the city.

M

MEDIA

Print

La Stampa, Il Corriere della Sera and *La Repubblica* are national papers with local sections, while the gossipy *La Nazione* is the region's paper favoured by most Florentines for its coverage of local news. English-language freebies include the fortnightly *The Florentine* (www.theflorentine.net) with excellent articles on Florence, Tuscany and Italy. *Firenze Spettacolo,* available from all newsstands, is the most informative monthly listings magazine.

Television and Radio

Television is deregulated in Italy. The Italian state TV network, RAI, broadcasts three channels which compete with various independent channels. There is also a vast number of radio stations, including many regional ones. Satellite gives access to CNN and BBC World in many hotels.

MONEY

In common with the other Eurozone countries of the EU, Italy's monetary unit is the euro (€), which is divided into 100 cents. Bank notes are issued in denominations of 5, 10, 20, 50, 100, 200 and 500 euros. Coins are denominated in 1 and 2 euros, and 1, 2, 5, 10, 20 and 50 cents.

Credit Cards

Most major credit cards, including Visa, American Express and Master-Card, are accepted in hotels, restaurants and shops, for air and train tickets, and for cash in any bank and some ATMs.

Banks, Exchange and ATMs

Changing money in a bank can be time-consuming, but the rates are generally better than in exchange offices. Exchange offices are found all over Florence, and at the train station.

P

POLICE

Italy has different types of police: the armed paramilitary *Carabinieri* who deal with serious violent crime; the state and municipal police who are responsible for day-to-day policing (including traffic); and a small unit of tourist police that deals with complaints and visitor safety. *See also Emergencies p.102.*

POST

The main post office in Florence is in Via Pellicceria 3 (near Piazza della Repubblica; www.poste.it), open Mon–Sat 8.15am–7pm. There are local post offices in each area of the city, generally open Mon–Fri 8.15am–1.30pm and Sat 8.15am–12.30pm.

Stamps *(francobolli)* are sold at post offices and tobacconists' shops *(tabacchi).*

Lost Property
There is a lost property office at Santa Maria Novella railway station.

Tipping
Some restaurants in Florence levy a *coperto* or cover charge so tipping is not expected unless you patronise very expensive hotels and restaurants. If you want to give a tip, leave the small change in a bar, leave 10 percent in a restaurant, and round up the taxi fare.

R

RELIGION

Although it has no official state religion, Italy is an overwhelmingly Catholic country, and the ideals and influence of the Vatican permeate Italian life and politics. While Tuscany is generally tolerant and accepting of other religions, religious and racial intolerance, especially against Roma and Muslims, is a growing problem in Italy, fomented by political parties such as the Lega Nord and Alleanza Nazionale.

T

TELEPHONES

Italy has a decreasing number of telephone kiosks, but almost every bar has a public phone. Telephone cards *(schede telefoniche)* – both Telecom Italia and other ones – can be purchased from tobacconists *(tabacchi)*, newsstands and other shops with the appropriate sticker in the window.

The international dialling code for Italy is 39, and the code for Florence is 055. Note that when calling from abroad you retain the initial zero on the local code. To call abroad from Italy, dial 00, then the country code (61 for Australia, 1 for Canada and the US, 353 for Ireland, 64 for New Zealand and 44 for the UK).

Mobile Phones

The EU set a cap on roaming charges in July 2012, bringing down the price of mobile telephone calls and texts within the EU, and another reduction will go into effect in July 2014. If your phone is 'unlocked' (contact your provider for details), it is straightforward to buy a local pay-as-you-go SIM card. The main providers are Vodafone Italia and Telecom Italia Mobile (TIM).

TIME ZONE

Italy is on Central European Time, 1 hour ahead of GMT. This means that if it is noon in Italy, it will be 11am in London and 6am in New York.

TOILETS

Public toilets are few and far between and not always clean and well maintained. All bars have toilet facilities, although visitors should at least buy a drink out of courtesy, if they want to use these facilities.

TOURIST INFORMATION

The Agenzia per il Turismo di Firenze (www.firenzeturismo.it) is Florence's efficient tourist information organisation. The most central office is Via Cavour 1r (tel: 055-290 832; Mon–Sat 8.30am–6.30pm, Sun 8.30am–1.30pm). Other offices are at Borgo

Above from far left: local *palazzo*; Neptune fountain.

Smoking
Smoking in enclosed public places is banned in Italy. The law is widely obeyed and hefty fines are given out to those who flaunt it.

Santa Croce 29r and Piazza Stazione.

In the UK, contact the Italian State Tourist Office (ENIT), located at 1 Princes Street, London W1B 2AY (tel: 020-7408 1254; www.enit.it).

In the US the Italian State Tourist Office is at 630 Fifth Avenue, Suite 1565, New York, NY 10111 (tel: 212-245 5618; www.enit.it).

TRANSPORT

The two main airports that serve Tuscany are Florence and Pisa. Florence's small **Peretola Airport** (also known as Amerigo Vespucci; www.aeroporto.firenze.it), is about 4km (2 miles) northwest of the city centre. From the UK the only direct flights are on Meridiana (www.meridiana.it) and British Airways (www.ba.com) both from London Gatwick _ although there are direct flights to Florence from elsewhere in Europe, including Frankfurt (Lufthansa) and Paris (Air France).

For most visitors flights to Pisa's **Galileo Galilei Airport** (www.pisa-airport.com), located 95km (59 miles) west of Florence, are the better option, being more frequent and usually cheaper than flights to Peretola. British Airways *(see above)*, Easyjet (www.easyjet.com), Ryanair (www.ryanair.com) and Jet2 (www.jet2.com) all fly here from the UK.

In the US, Delta (www.delta.com) flies direct from New York, JFK, to

Pisa from May to October. Alternatively the best routes are via London, Brussels, Paris or Frankfurt; or to fly direct to Milan or Rome; the excellent airport train linking Rome's Fiumicino Airport with Termini station (in central Rome) and frequent, fast trains to Florence make this a good option for visitors from the US.

Arrival

Florence's Peretola Airport is connected to the city centre every 30 minutes by the Ataf-Sita (www.ataf.net) airport shuttle bus to Santa Maria Novella railway station. The journey time is about 20 minutes, and tickets are available on the bus. A taxi into the centre of Florence will cost around €20-25 and takes approximately 15 minutes.

From Pisa airport the simplest option is to take the Terravision coach (www.terravision.eu) with departures timed to coincide with flights. The journey time is 75 minutes. Alternatively you can take a train from Pisa airport station to Florence, or the more regular train service (www.trenitalia.it) which links Florence to Pisa Centrale station, rapidly reached from the airport by train, bus or taxi. Allow 70-80 minutes for the whole journey.

By Rail

The train journey from London to Florence via Paris takes around 13-18 hours via Paris and Turin or Milan. For

Cycling

Cycling is becoming increasingly popular among Florentines and there is an increasing number of bike lanes. However cyclists need their wits about them to steer a course through the hordes of tourists around the Duomo. Bicycles can be hired from Alinari (Via Zanobi 38r; tel: 055-280 500; www.alinarirental.com) and Florence by Bike (Via San Zanobi 120r; tel: 055-480 814; www.florencebybike.it). Two-hour guided bike tours, from March to October daily at 10am and 3pm, are organized by Florence Town I Bike (www.florencetown.com).

international rail information contact Rail Europe (www.raileurope.com).

Public Transport

The centre of Florence is small enough to cover on foot and given the heart of the city is now banned to traffic, buses included, this is the easiest way to see the city. However if you want to cross the town by public transport or visit peripheral sights there are fast and efficient electric buses (C1, C2, C3 and D) stopping near the main sights.

The local bus network, which also provides an efficient service out to suburbs such as Fiesole, is ATAF (Piazza Stazione, www.ataf.net). Tickets can be bought from tobacconists *(tabacchi)*, newsstands, bars, and from ATAF offices or automatic ticket machines at main points throughout the city, including the main transport hub of Santa Maria Novella station. You can purchase a ticket on board the bus but it will cost a good deal more. With the 90-minute ticket (€1.20) you can make as many journeys as you like. The *biglietto multiplo* consists of four single 90-minute tickets, and the 3-hour, 24-hour, 3-day and 7-day tickets are self-explanatory. All tickets must be stamped in the appropriate machines on board the bus at the beginning of the first journey.

The controversial new tramline network has one line open, from Santa Maria Novella to Scandicci in the southwest of the city, a route rarely taken by tourists.

Taxis

Taxis are white, and are hired from ranks in the main squares and at the station. They seldom stop if you hail them in the street. Taxis have meters and are also required to display fares on tariff cards. The radio taxi system is fast and efficient (tel: 055-4390 or 4242).

Driving and Car Hire

Florence has a city-centre driving ban and cars must be left in the car parks on the edge of the centre (www.firenze parcheggi.it). You can rent cars from major companies (Hertz, Avis, Europcar, etc). Traffic travels on the right-hand side of the road, and seat belts are compulsory. Note that ALT is a stop line painted on the road at junctions; STOP is for a pedestrian crossing.

V

VISAS AND PASSPORTS

Citizens from EU countries require a passport or a Visitor's Identification Card to enter Italy. A visa is not required. Holders of passports from most other countries do not require visas for stays of fewer than three months, except for nationals of some Eastern European countries, who need to obtain visas from the Italian Embassy in their own country.

Above from far left: prints at Pucci; glorious views over the city and the Tuscan hills.

Parking

Parking is a major problem in Florence; the safest place is in one of the costly private underground car parks found all over the city. Cheaper, but still with surveillance cameras, are the city car parks (www.firenze parcheggi.it). Street parking is almost impossible, as most central areas are strictly no-parking. Public street parking is marked by blue stripes on the road, and these must be paid for by the hour. There are now some parking meters in the city. Do not leave your car on a space next to a *passo carrabile* or a *sosta vietato* sign or in a disabled space (marked in yellow).

Florence is not a cheap destination when it comes to accommodation, but you definitely get what you pay for. That said, prices can drop considerably outside high season (Christmas, Easter and the summer months), and it is worth asking to see what discounts are available. The city does tend to get booked up very quickly – not surprising considering the high numbers of visitors – so if you have your heart set on a particular place, be sure to book well in advance of your trip.

Places to stay in the city range from sumptuous *palazzo* and boutique hotels to simple but charming B&Bs. Generally, the most expensive hotels are found along the banks of the river with the cheapest accommodation clustered around Santa Maria Novella and San Lorenzo. For a bit of peace and quiet, the villas of Oltrarno and Fiesole are wonderful. If the listings below are fully booked, then the Florence Agenzia per il Turismo website (www.firenzeturismo.it), with its wide array of accommodation, is a useful place to search and make bookings.

Florence introduced a tourist or accommodation tax in 2011. Guests are charged €1–5 a night according to the hotel's number of stars. Thus a couple staying four nights in a 4-star hotel would have to pay an extra €32 (payable in cash only). The charge is for a maximum of 10 nights, and children under 10 are exempt.

The Duomo

Brunelleschi
Piazza Santa Elisabetta 3; tel: 055-27370; www.hotelbrunelleschi.it; €€€€
This comfortable four-star hotel is located in a tiny central piazza and partly housed in a church with a 6th-century tower.

Guelfo Bianco
Via Cavour 29; tel: 055-288 330; www.ilguelfobianco.it; €€
A good option for such a central location, with nicely furnished rooms in two adjacent 15th-century houses just north of the Duomo.

Piazza della Signoria

Continentale
Vicolo dell'Oro 6r; tel: 055-27262; www.lungarnocollection.com; €€€€
Chic retro-style hotel with appealing designer features, wooden-floored rooms, comfortable beds and Venetian blinds. Adding to the mix is top-class service and a panoramic terrace.

Hermitage
Vicolo Marzio 1, Piazza del Pesce;

Price guide for a double room for one night in high season:

€€€€	over 300 euros
€€€	150–300 euros
€€	100–150 euros
€	below 100 euros

tel: 055-287 216; www.hermitage hotel.com; €€€

A delightful hotel located directly above the Ponte Vecchio, with a lovely roof garden overlooking the city. Some of the (rather small) rooms have wonderful river views, although for sleeping you may prefer to stay in one of the quieter ones at the back.

NH Porta Rossa

Via Porta Rossa 19; tel: 055-271 0901; www.nh-hotels.com; €€–€€€

The family-run Porta Rossa hotel in an ancient *palazzo* has been taken over by the Spanish chain NH Hotels, but manages to retain at least some of its old Florentine charm. Rooms are good value for a 4-star hotel in the centre.

Relais Uffizi

Chiasso de' Baroncelli 16; tel: 055-267 6239; www.relaisuffizi.it; €€

This tiny hotel is tucked away behind the Galleria degli Uffizi, with spectacular views over Piazza della Signoria and the Palazzo Vecchio. The rooms are quite traditional in character and some have four-poster beds.

Torre Guelfa

Borgo SS Apostoli 8; tel: 055-239 6338; www.hoteltorreguelfa.com; €€

Part of this hotel includes the tallest privately owned tower (built in 1280) in Florence. There are pretty furnishings in bedrooms, and smart bathrooms, but the winner is the building itself.

Santa Croce

Grand Cavour

Via del Proconsolo 3; tel: 055-266 271; www.hotelcavour.com; €€€

A recently modernised luxury hotel in the historic 14th-century Palazzo Strozzi-Ridolfi. It is in a quiet location and has fine city views from the intimate roof garden. Compared to some of the other *palazzo* hotels in the city, the rates here are quite reasonable.

J&J

Via di Mezzo 20; tel: 055-26312; www.jandjhotel.net; €€€

Housed in a former convent near Sant' Ambrogio, this smart and discreet hotel has been given a design feel. To add to the style, breakfast is served in the cloister in summer. The rooms are very comfortable; some are enormous.

Monna Lisa

Borgo Pinti 27; tel: 055-247 9751; www.monnalisa.it; €€€

A small, but in part characterful, hotel set in a 14th-century *palazzo*, furnished with paintings and antiques. The quieter rooms, overlooking the delightful courtyard garden, are the best. Try to avoid the rather charmless rooms in the extension.

Regency

Piazza Massimo d'Azeglio 3; tel: 055-245247; www.regency-hotel.com; €€€€

Above from far left: painted ceiling and bar at the Tornabuoni Beacci *(see p.112).*

This is a grand hotel in a 19th-century *palazzo*, with a highly regarded restaurant and an elegant garden set between the two wings. The rooms are elegant and comfortable with good facilities.

Villa Liana
Via Alfieri 18; tel: 055-245 303; www.hotelliana.com; €€
A quiet, pleasant and slightly faded hotel some way north of the centre in the former British Embassy building. The rooms range from the clean and simple to the elegant 'Count's Room'.

Piazza della Repubblica

Antica Torre di Via Tornabuoni
Via de'Tornabuoni 1; tel: 055-265 8161; www.tornabuoni1.com; €€€
The rooms and apartments here are luxuriously comfortable, and all are set on the 4th, 5th and 6th floors of a medieval *palazzo* overlooking Piazza Santa Trinità, with bird's-eye views of the city and, from some, the river.

Helvetia & Bristol
Via dei Pescioni 2; tel: 055-26651; www.royaldemeure.com; €€€€
A small but grand hotel, with antiques and paintings scattered around the rooms and hallways. The sumptuous rooms have wonderful views, and the marble-clad bathrooms are a treat. The hotel has a good restaurant and a pretty winter garden.

Tornabuoni Beacci
Via de'Tornabuoni 3; tel: 055-212 645; www.tornabuonihotels.com; €€€
A lovely hotel, set in a 14th-century *palazzo* in the city's most prestigious shopping street. The rooms are nicely old fashioned with solid furnishings. All in all, the place exudes an appealing old-world charm.

San Lorenzo

Botticelli
Via Taddea 8; tel: 055-290 905; www.hotelbotticelliflorence.com; €€
Located at the back of the central market, this hotel is both comfortable and appealing, with all mod cons alongside original architectural features such as vaulted ceilings and the odd fresco.

Casci
Via Cavour 13; tel: 055-211 686; www.hotelcasciflorence.com; €–€€
Situated north of the San Lorenzo market area, this frescoed Quattrocento *palazzo* is family-run, with a welcoming atmosphere. Guest rooms are simply but pleasantly furnished, and look out onto the courtyard, small side streets or gardens.

Centro
Via dei Ginori 17; tel: 055-230 2901; www.hotelcentro.net; €€
A historic place to stay, near the Via Cavour and the Palazzo Medici-

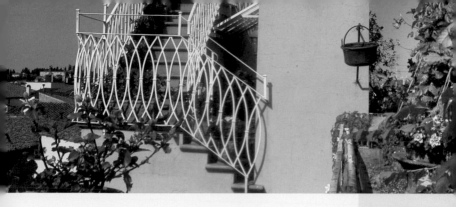

Riccardi. This grand *palazzo* was once Raphael's residence and has now been renovated to provide spacious, light rooms for guests.

Residenza Johanna 1

Via Bonifacio Lupi 14; tel: 055-481 896; www.johanna.it; €

One of a set of great-value-for-money places to stay in Florence. Set in a residential area to the northwest of the centre, the rooms are comfortable and nicely decorated, but there are few hotel frills.

San Marco

Antica Dimora Johlea

Via San Gallo 80/76; tel: 055-463 3292; www.johanna.it; €–€€

An excellent-value place to stay (part of a good-value chain), not too far from the centre. The two residences here are set in the area around the church of San Marco. They retain an authentic Tuscan feel and have comfortable, individually decorated rooms.

Four Seasons Firenze

Borgo Pinti 99; tel: 055-26261; www. fourseasons.com/florence; €€€€

This über-luxurious *palazzo* hotel is stunning, with frescoed ceilings, sumptuous furnishings and delightful gardens. None of this is cheap, but staying here is certainly doing Florence in style. The bar and restaurant are also worth checking out for a cocktail or blow-out dinner.

Loggiato dei Serviti

Piazza della Santissima Annunziata 3; tel: 055-26312; www.loggiato deiservitihotel.it; €€€

A fabulous place to stay and part of the historic fabric of the city. San Gallo's gracious 16th-century *palazzo* is set on a lovely traffic-free piazza and looks out onto Brunelleschi's Ospedale degli Innocenti. Antiques adorn the vaulted interior, and the rooms are all beautifully decorated.

Morandi alla Crocetta

Via Laura 50; tel: 055-234 4747; www.hotelmorandi.it; €€–€€€

This is a quiet, informal hotel housed in an ex-convent. The 10 peaceful rooms are comfortable and furnished with a few antiques. Several of them have their own private terraces – ask for one of those if the budget allows.

Santa Maria Novella

Albion

Via Il Prato 22r; tel: 055-214 171; www.hotelalbion.it; €€

Set in a stylish neo-Gothic *palazzo*, the hotel is a showcase for modern art. The rooms are decent, and free bicycles are available for guests.

Hotel Baglioni

Piazza dell'Unità Italiana 6; tel: 055-23580; www.hotelbaglioni.it; €€€

This classic hotel retains its air of discreet elegance while providing extremely comfortable rooms. The

Above from far left: room keys and terrace at the Tornabuoni Beacci hotel.

rooftop restaurant has fabulous views of the city skyline. Popular with the business community.

Casa Howard
Via della Scala 18; tel: 06-6992 4555; www.casahoward.com; €€€
A stylish guesthouse, offering upmarket rooms in a fine old mansion; each of the 12 is decorated in a striking individual style, with bold colours contrasting with antiques and old furniture. Great location too, next to the Officina di Santa Maria Novella.

Grand Hotel Minerva
Piazza Santa Maria Novella 16; tel: 055-27230; www.grandhotel minerva.com; €€€€
One of the few centrally located hotels with a pool, and what's more, it's a rooftop pool with views to die for. Aside from this, the rooms are quietly luxurious, and the service is excellent.

J.K. Place
Piazza Santa Maria Novella 7; tel: 055-264 5181; www.jkplace.com; €€€€
This chic and luxurious hotel is tucked into the corner of Piazza Santa Maria Novella. The elegant interiors contain works of art and classic designer furniture and lighting. The suites and penthouse are particularly impressive, and the terrace bar is wonderful.

Mario's
Via Faenza 89; tel: 055-216 801; www.hotelmarios.com; €–€€
Most of the hotels in Via Faenza near the Mercato Centrale are scruffy, but Mario's is an exception. It's decorated in rustic Tuscan style, with comfortable bedrooms (the back is quieter) and a pretty breakfast room.

Palazzo dal Borgo
Via della Scala 6; tel: 055-216 237; www.hotelaprile.it; €€€
Formerly the Hotel Aprile, this has been revamped into an elegant four-star hotel. More appealing than most hotels near the station, it is an ex-Medici palace complete with frescoes, a pleasant breakfast room and pretty courtyard.

St Regis
Piazza Ognissanti 1; tel: 055-27161; www.stregisflorence.com; €€€€
On the Arno, the 5-star St Regis (formerly the Grand) reopened in 2011 after a major revamp. Expect polished service, luxurious guest rooms, gourmet cuisine and fine river views – with prices to match.

Oltrarno

Annalena
Via Romana 34; tel: 055-222 402; www.hotelannalena.it; €–€€
Great-value antique-furnished rooms in a gracious 15th-century convent that was originally built as a refuge

for widows of the Florentine nobility. Located near the Boboli Garden, with views over a pretty garden.

Lungarno

Borgo San Jacopo 14; tel: 055-27261; www.lungarnocollection. com; €€€–€€€€

Smart, comfortable modern hotel popular for its superb position on the river and views of the Ponte Vecchio from the front rooms. There is also a restaurant specialising in fish.

Torre di Bellosguardo

Via Roti Michelozzi 2; tel: 055-229 8145; www.torrebellosguardo.com; €€€

Set in the hills just above Porta Romana, this quiet, atmospheric and roomy hotel consists of a 14th-century tower attached to a 16th-century villa. It has frescoed reception rooms and charmingly decorated bedrooms, with antiques and quirky details. It has a secluded swimming pool and lovely grounds with a lily pond.

Villa Cora

Viale Machiavelli 18; tel: 055-229 8451; www.whythebesthotels.com; €€€€

This 19th-century villa on the avenue leading up to Piazzale Michelangelo underwent a major refurbishment, reopening in 2010. It is now better than ever with lavish public rooms, extensive gardens, a heated pool in the park, spa, gym and gastronomic restaurant.

Villa Liberty

Viale Michelangelo 40; tel: 055-681 0581; www.hotelflorenceliberty.com; €€€

Situated in a chic residential area of Florence that winds up towards Piazzale Michelangelo, this early 20th-century villa – set in a lovely garden – is cosy with slighty kitsch rooms.

Hotel Villa La Vedetta

Viale Michelangelo 78; tel: 055-681 631; www.villalavedettahotel.com; €€€€

Five-star luxury in a neo-Renaissance villa near the Ponte Vecchio. From the pool is a panoramic view of the city, dominated by Brunelleschi's dome.

Fiesole

Pensione Bencistà

Via Benedetto da Maiano 4; tel: 055-59163; www.bencista.com; €€

Set on the Florence road just south of Fiesole, this delightful 14th-century villa lives up to its name, which means 'stay well'. The grand interior of the sprawling building is full of antiques and rustic furnishings. There are cosy reception rooms, fine hillside views and, in the warmer seasons, breakfast is served alfresco on the lovely terrace. The *pensione* now has a wellness centre, and a swimming pool for 2013.

Above from far left: traditional style is typical in Florence; smart room-service menu.

Dining is an important event in Florence. Once a languid affair, lunch during the working week is increasingly treated as a lighter snack, as more businesses remain open through the lunch hour, and Florentines become more health-conscious. On a Sunday, however, the midday meal is given great importance and may continue well into the afternoon. In the evening, Florentines usually eat at around 8.30pm.

The Duomo

Alle Murate
Via del Proconsolo 16r; tel: 055-240 618; Tue–Sun 7.30–11pm; €€€€
This high-class restaurant is located in a *palazzo* with frescoed vaults. Chef Giovanni Iorio, who has been cooking here for 30 years, offers a creative twist on Tuscan food, using top quality seasonal produce. Reserve.

Coquinarius
Via delle Oche 15r; tel: 055-230 2153; Mon–Sat 9am–late; €€
This tiny yet fashionable *enoteca* is always full, and has a great selection of wines. You can eat here at almost any time of day. Try the lunch salads, the *carpaccio*, platters of cheese and cured meats or the rightfully famous pear and pecorino ravioli. Save space for the exquisite homemade desserts.

Oleum Olivae
Via Sant'Egidio 22r; tel: 055-200 1092; Mon–Fri 11am–6pm; €–€€
Order a glass of wine and pick your *panino* bread, filling and sauce from the delicatessen – one good choice is the pecorino garnished with rocket and walnut sauce. Get there early to avoid the long queues.

Piazza della Signoria

Antico Fattore
Via Lambertesca 1/3r; tel: 055-288 975; Mon–Sat 12.15–3pm, 7.15–10.30pm; €€
This traditional *trattoria* offers good meat and game dishes as well as the standard Tuscan and Florentine fare such as *trippa* (tripe) and *ribollita* (vegetable and bread soup).

Oliviero
Via delle Terme 51r; tel: 055-212 421; Mon–Sat 7.30–11pm; €€€
Historic, sophisticated restaurant that markets itself as being part of the *dolce vita fiorentina* (Florentine good life), this was a former haunt of Lisa Minelli, Sophia Loren and Federico Fellini. The menu changes every couple of months, and everything is prepared freshly in house.

Price guide for a two-course meal for one with a glass of house wine:

€€€€	over 60 euros
€€€	40–60 euros
€€	25–40 euros
€	below 25 euros

Ora d'Aria

Via dei Georgofili, 11r; tel: 055-200 1619; Tue–Sat 12.30–2.30pm, 7.30–10pm, Mon 7.30–10pm; www.oradariaristorante.com; €€–€€€

In its new location, very handy for the Uffizi, this is a fashionable little restaurant renowned for light contemporary variations on classic Tuscan fare. Reservations recommended (at least 24 hours prior to arrival).

Santa Croce

Acqua al Due

Via della Vigna Vecchia 40r; tel: 055-284 170; daily 7.30pm–1am; €€

A real dining experience, which requires booking ahead due to its popularity. If you have a big appetite, try the *assaggi di primi* (five pasta dishes chosen by the chef) followed by the *assaggi di dolci* (a selection of the desserts of the day).

Antico Noè

Volta di San Pietro 6r; tel: 055-234 0838; Mon–Sat 8am–midnight; €

Tiny place that offers authentic Tuscan food at low prices as well as 20 different *panini*. The delicious *tagliatelle ai porcini* (mushroom pasta) is recommended.

Baldovino Trattoria

Via di San Giuseppe 22r; tel: 055-241 773; daily noon–2.30pm, 7–10.30pm; €€

This place offers a little bit of everything Italian: great pasta, pizzas, salads and a few more elaborate dishes on top. A welcome change from traditional Florentine restaurants.

Caffè Italiano Osteria

Via Isola delle Stinche 11/13r; tel: 055-289 368; Tue–Sun 10am–1am; €€€

Set inside the 14th-century Salviati Palace, with a changing menu of high-quality Tuscan cuisine, this attractive space with its rough wooden tables is one of the nicest in the city. As well as very decent wines by the glass the simple but imaginative food, such as the cold tripe salad, is well done and tasty. Try the huge Florentine *bistecca* to share.

Caffè and Osteria de' Benci

Via dei Benci 13r; tel: 055-216 887 (Caffè), 055-234 4923 (Osteria); Mon–Sat 12.30–3.30pm, 7.30–11pm; €€

A small, relaxed café, where drinks and *panini* are served from the early morning to the late evening, and a next-door *osteria* with more substantial local dishes.

Cantinetta Antinori

Piazza Antinori 3 (off Via de' Tornabuoni); tel: 055-292 234; Mon–Fri 12–2.30pm, 7–10.30pm; www.cantinetta-antinori.com; €€–€€€

Above from far left: typically rich Florentine dessert; lunch at a local *ristorante*; piles of tempting nougat.

Part of the Antinori wine empire and set on the ground floor of Palazzo Antinori, this is an upmarket wine bar with dark wood furnishings and simple Tuscan cuisine. Much of the produce, and the wines of course, come from the Antinori estate.

Cibrèo

Via del Verrocchio 8r; tel: 055-234 1100; Tue–Sat 12.50–2.30pm, 7.30–11pm; €€€€

This justly famous restaurant is elegant yet relaxed and one of the most popular with visitors and Florentines alike. The food of chef Fabio Picchi is Tuscan with an innovative twist. Eat much the same food but for a cheaper price in the Cibrèino *trattoria*, which is entered from Piazza Ghiberti.

Enoteca Pinchiorri

Via Ghibellina 87; tel: 055-242 777; Tue–Sat 7.30–10pm; www.enoteca pinchiorri.com; €€€€

A foodie's paradise, Enoteca Pinchiorri is garlanded with awards – it has been hailed by some as one of the best restaurants in Europe, although scorned by others as pretentious. The only way to find out is by taking your credit card and diving in. Offers Tuscan food with a French influence and an outstanding wine list. Booking essential.

Finisterrae

Via de' Pepi 6; tel: 055-263 8675;

Tue–Sun noon–3pm, 7.30pm–1am; €€–€€€

A Mediterranean bar and restaurant with a choice selection of food from various cuisines. Start with tapas, followed by a Moroccan-style *tagine* or pasta dish. The ambience is relaxed and sultry, especially in the bar area.

Il Pizzaiuolo

Via dei Macci 113r; tel: 055-241 171; Sept–Jul: Mon–Sat 12.30–2.30pm, 7.30pm–12.30am; €–€€

The pizzas here are Neapolitan-style wonders. There are lots more dishes besides, including mixed *antipasti*.

La Botte

Via di San Giuseppe 18r; tel: 055-247 6420; daily noon–11pm, closed Mon eve off season; €–€€

This is the only bar in Florence to use enomatic technology to offer a wide selection of wines by the glass, half-glass or *in assaggio* – just a taste. Customers use a wine card and can choose from 64 varieties. Food is tapas-style with salamis, prosciutto and Tuscan street food. The bar is run by David Gardner following the success of his Baldovino Trattoria (*see page 117*).

La Giostra

Borgo Pinti 12r; tel: 055-241 341; Mon–Sat 1–2.30pm, 7pm–late, Sun 7pm–late; €€€

This is a renowned restaurant run by a Habsburg prince. The *crostini* are

Above from far left: expect to find excellent grappas in Tuscany; simply prepared pasta.

delicious, as are the handmade pasta dishes. White truffles are on offer in season, and they do a mean Wiener Schnitzel and Sacher Torte.

La Pentola dell'Oro

Via di Mezzo 24/26r; tel: 055-241 808; Sept–Jul: Mon–Sat 7.30pm–midnight; €€–€€€

As well as being unique, this is one of the friendliest restaurants in the city. Chef Giuseppe Alessi is more than willing to explain the dishes, many of which are inspired by medieval and Renaissance Tuscan cuisine.

Targa

Lungarno Colombo 7; tel: 055-677 377; Mon–Sat 12.30–2.30pm, 8–10.45pm; €€€

This bistro, run by chef Gabriele Tarchiani, has a delightful riverside setting. The traditional Tuscan food is given a creative edge and there are some excellent fish dishes.

Piazza della Repubblica

Chiaro Scuro

Via del Corso 13r; tel: 055-214 227; Mon–Sat 7.30am–8.30pm; €

This café has coffee from all over the world, as well as flavoured hot chocolates, cocktails, a buffet lunch and one of the best *aperitivo* buffets in Florence.

Il Paiolo

Via del Corso 42r; tel: 055-215 019; Mon noon–3pm, Tue–Sat

noon–3pm, 7–10.30pm; €€

A cosy restaurant that serves good-quality pan-Italian food. The fresh fish and homemade desserts are the highlights.

Perché No?

Via de' Tavolini 19r; tel: 055-239 8969; Wed–Mon 11am–11pm, Tue noon–8pm; €

One of the oldest ice cream parlours in town and a pioneer of the *semifreddo* – a mousse-like *gelato* that is perfect for colder days.

San Lorenzo

Giannino in San Lorenzo

Borgo San Lorenzo 35/37r; tel: 055-239 9799; daily 12.30–3pm, 7.30–10pm; €€

One of the better restaurants in this area, offering traditional food such as *bistecca alla fiorentina* and *ribollita* and a good wine selection. Special themed evenings are worth looking out for.

Lobs

Via Faenza 75r; tel: 055-212 748; daily 7–11.30pm; €€€

One of the best fish restaurants in Florence, Lobs offers a range of seafood including swordfish, prawns, octopus and oysters. The lobster should be ordered in advance.

Trattoria Zàrà

Piazza del Mercato Centrale 26r; tel:

055-215 411; daily noon–3pm, 7pm–1am; €€–€€€

Set in the piazza behind the market, this lively taverna-like *trattoria* offers pizzas and pasta, meat and fish-based dishes, and a good choice of wines.

San Marco

Il Vegetariano

Via delle Ruote 30r; tel: 055-475 030; Tue–Fri 12.30–2.30pm, 7.30pm–midnight, Sat–Sun 7.30pm–midnight; €

This restaurant's use of the freshest vegetables in its dishes makes it the main contender for the city's best vegetarian eatery, although, admittedly, there are few of those in Florence from which to choose. Informal and unassuming.

Pugi

Piazza San Marco 9b; tel: 055-280 981; Mon–Sat 7.45am–8pm; €

Famous among Florentines for its *schiacciate* (flat breads of various kinds). Buy *focaccia* or pizza by weight as a snack or for lunch on the run.

Ristorante da Mimmo

Via San Gallo 57/59r; tel: 055-481 030; Mon–Sat 12.30–2pm, 7.30–10pm; €€

Located within a former theatre, this place offers good food and wine at affordable prices. There's a changing menu, which is often inspired by southern Italian cooking.

Taverna del Bronzino

Via delle Ruote 27r; tel: 055-495 220; Mon–Sat 12.30–2.30pm, 7.30–10.30pm; €€€–€€€€

A variety of European cuisines served in an elegant restaurant with a vaulted ceiling and patio. Try the *ravioli alla senese* (ricotta-and-spinach-filled pasta) or one of the less Italian but equally divine dishes.

Santa Maria Novella

Buca Lapi

Via del Trebbio 1r; tel: 055-213 768; Mon–Sat 7–10.30pm; €€€

In the cellar of the Palazzo Antinori, this lovely restaurant is regarded as serving one of the best *bistecca alla fiorentina* (enormous and beautifully grilled). As expected, being in the basement of the *palazzo* of one of Tuscany's best wine producers, it has an excellent range of wines.

Il Latini

Via del Palchetti 6r; tel: 055-210 916; Tue–Sun 12.30–2.30pm, 7.30–10.30pm; €€

Expect to queue to get into this sprawling noisy eatery with communal tables. The Tuscan food is good and filling, and the ambience is convivial and fun.

La Carabaccia

Via Palazzuolo 190r; tel: 055-214 782; daily noon–3pm, 7–11pm; €€€

Set in a renovated old tavern, La

Carabaccia offers a daily and seasonal menu using the freshest ingredients. The specialities include grilled meats cooked on charcoal and traditional Tuscan dishes. The excellent food is supplemented by a stone cellar full of the best Tuscan wines – they also make their own basil liqueur. The setting is a medieval Florentine dining room, complete with original features.

Trattoria Sostanza

Via del Porcellana 25r; tel: 055-212 619; Mon–Fri noon–2.15pm, 7.30–9.45pm; €€

Relaxed restaurant with basic decor and communal seating, offering traditional Tuscan dishes including *tortellini in brodo* (*tortellini* in broth). Concessions are not made for tourists, and some basic Italian would be useful. However, this is a true Florentine dining experience: substantial and satisfying food. No credit cards.

Oltrarno

Antico Ristoro di' Cambi

Via Sant' Onofrio 1r; tel: 055-217 134; Mon–Sat 12.15–2.30pm, 7.30–10.30pm; €

This popular restaurant fits perfectly into the heart of the bustling San Frediano area. Traditional in feel and food, it offers excellent Tuscan cooking and no-nonsense service.

Bevo Vino

Via di San Niccolò 59r; tel: 055-200 1709; daily noon–1am; €

A lovely medium-sized *enoteca*, offering daily specials for first and second courses, plus *carpaccio* and *bruschetta*. Good wine and cheese selections, and the service is friendly and knowledgeable. Outdoor seating is available in the summer.

Filipepe

Via di San Niccolò 39r; tel: 055-200 1397; daily 12.30–2.30pm, 7.30–11pm; €€€

Filipepe offers an elegant take on modern Mediterranean cuisine. Soft candle lighting, cove ceilings, and the bottles of wine lining the walls give each area a private yet comfortable feel. The menu offers a seasonal selection of ingredients, frequently from the southern regions of Italy, including different kinds of *carpaccio*, salads, soups and pastas. There is a small outdoor area for meals in summer.

Quattro Leoni

Piazza della Passera, Via de' Vellutini 1r; tel: 055-218 562; daily noon–2pm, 7–10.30pm; €€

One of the city's oldest restaurants, founded in 1550, this eatery is in a quiet square where diners can sit outside during the summer. The traditional cooking is excellent and there are new additions to the Tuscan menu on a daily basis.

Above from far left: serving up spaghetti carbonara; rustic oven-baked pizza; Tuscan stew.

NIGHTLIFE

In Florence the main theatres listed below not only put on seasons of music, opera and dance but also plays, generally in Italian, and other events throughout the year. For many visitors nightlife amounts to no more than a meal out, a stroll through the floodlit centre and a drink or two to end off the evening. Florence is not renowned for nightclubs but has a good number of bars, often with live music. Classical concerts are held in churches year-round, and in summer piazzas are the stage for a variety of performers, classical and contemporary.

Theatre

Teatro Communale
Corso Italia 16; tel: 055-277 9350; www.maggiofiorentino.com
The main theatre for the Maggio Musicale festival, the Teatro Communale also puts on a full programme of concerts, operas and other events year round (book online or in person at the box office).

Teatro Goldoni
Via Santa Maria 15; tel: 055-210 804; www.goldoniteatro.it
This small, attractive 18th-century theatre in Oltrarno is used for some performances during the Maggio as well as shows for the Florence Dance Festival (www.florencedance.org).

Teatro della Pergola
Via della Pergola 18–32; tel: 055-226 4353; www.fondazioneteatro dellapergola.it
This beautiful 17th-century theatre hosts a world-class chamber music season organised by the Amici della Musica (www.amicimusica.fi.it) as well as plays by noted Italian companies, chamber concerts and some opera.

Teatro Puccini
Via delle Cascine 41; tel: 055-362 067; www.teatropuccini.it
This theatre on the outskirts of town once served as a cinema but now hosts seasons of plays as well as the occasional opera. Built in 1939–40 it is one of the most impressive examples of Fascist-era architecture in the city.

Teatro del Sale
Via dei Macci 111; tel: 055-200 1492; Tue–Sat from 7.30pm; www. edizioniteatrodelsalecibreofirenze.it
This old theatre northeast of Santa Croce provides a novel experience,

Fiesole

Fiesole's Roman Amphitheatre (Teatro Romano), features heavily in the town's annual summer festival, Estate Fiesolana (mid-June–Aug), when it is used to stage open-air performances of concerts, ballet, drama and film. See www.estatefiesolana.it for further information.

combining theatre with dinner. Fabio Picchi (of the Cibrèo emporium, *see p.118*) produces Tuscan dishes, buffet-style on the theatre stage. The tables are then taken away and the show begins. The dinner is a fixed affordable price, with a small fee for the theatre membership. Reservations are required.

Teatro Verdi
Via Ghibellina 99; tel: 055-212 320; www.teatroverdionline.it
The vast Teatro Verdi is the venue for light opera, ballet, jazz and rock concerts. The Orchestra Regionale Toscana's lively concert series is held here and runs from December to May.

Cinema
Odeon
Piazza Strozzi 2; tel: 055-295 051; www.odeon.intoscana.it
Just west of Piazza della Repubblica, this is one of the few cinemas in Florence that regularly shows films in their original language. Films in English are shown on Monday, Tuesday and Thursday (known as 'Odeon Original Sound nights'). At other times the programme includes a mix of Italian and dubbed films.

Bars and Live Music
Dolce Vita
Piazza del Carmine; tel: 055-284 595; www.dolcevitaflorence.com
This fashionable, arty bar-club in the

Oltrarno quarter draws the crowds during happy hour and for after dinner drinks. *Aperitivi* come with a generous buffet and you can sit outside at tables overlooking Carmine church. Live music twice a week from 7.30-9.30pm, followed by a DJ until the early hours of the morning.

Ganzo
Via dei Macci 85r; tel: 055-21076; www.ganzoflorence.it
Ganzo is Tuscan for 'cool' and this is a new bar and club for the arts, with lectures, exhibitions and culinary events.

Moyo
Via dei Benci 23r; tel: 055-247 9738; www.moyo.it
This swanky cocktail bar in the Santa Croce area offers a good buffet for the price of your cocktail (buffet served 7-10.30pm, with dancing later). Weekly themes might include a sushi buffet or Mexico *aperitivo* and Latin party. It is open all day for drinks and light meals, and has free WiFi.

Zoe
Via de Renai 13r; tel: 055-243 111; www.zoebar.it
This is a popular and stylish spot for summer evening cocktails, with an aperitif buffet and DJ music. It's also open throughout the day for snacks and light meals.

Above from far left: Teatro Goldoni; Dolce Vita.

Listings
Firenze Spettacolo, available from all newsstands, is the most informative monthly listings magazine for nightlife, clubs, bars, restaurants and the live arts in Florence. The tourist office at Via Cavour 1r provides free listings of current musical events.

CREDITS

Insight Step by Step Florence
Written by: Maria Lord and Christopher Catling
Updated by: Susie Boulton
Commissioning Editor: Catherine Dreghorn
Series Editor: Carine Tracanelli
Cartographic Production: original cartography Berndtson & Berndtson, updated by Apa Cartography Department
Design: Richard Cooke
Production: Tynan Dean

Photography:
All Pictures © Britta Jaschinski/APA except:
Bridgeman Art Library 22T; Chris Coe 49; istockphoto 20T, 42T, 86, 87, 89; Jerry Dennis/APA 1, 8TL, 24–5, 37, 48, 51, 70; Mockford & Bonetti 8–9, 8BL, 8BR, 12, 13, 13B, 14, 24CB, 27, 31, 40, 55, 77, 85, 88, 90, 90–1, 96; Corbis 2MR, 13BR, 21, 64, 122; Fotolia 2-3, 8–9, 24-25, 98-99; Scala 44, 45, 82, 83, 84B, 92, 93, 94, 96/97; Topfoto 23T.
Front cover: main image: 4Corners; small images: fotolia.
Back cover: fotolia.

Printed by: CTPS - China.

Second Edition 2013

CONTACTING THE EDITORS

We would appreciate it if readers would alert us to errors or outdated information by writing to us at insight@apaguide.co.uk or APA Publications, PO Box 7910, London SE1 1WE, UK.

www.insightguides.com

DISTRIBUTION

Worldwide

APA Publications GmbH & Co. Verlag KG
(Singapore branch)
7030 Ang Mo Kio Ave 5
08-65 Northstar @ AMK
Singapore 569880
Email: apasin@singnet.com.sg

UK and Ireland

Dorling Kindersley Ltd,
a Penguin Group company
80 Strand, London
WC2R 0RL, UK
Email: customerservice@dk.com

US

Ingram Publisher Services
One Ingram Blvd, PO Box 3006
La Vergne, TN 37086-1986
Email: customer.service@ingrampublisher
services.com

Australia

Universal Publishers
PO Box 307
St. Leonards, NSW 1590
Email: sales@universalpublishers.com.au

New Zealand

Brown Knows Publications
11 Artesia Close, Shamrock Park
Auckland, New Zealand 2016
Email: sales@brownknows.co.nz

INDEX